Cleveland Way

T0317976

Alan Staniforth lives at Robin Hood's Bay
on the Cleveland Way. He worked for the
North York Moors National Park Authority
for thirty years, firstly as an Information
Officer and later as Heritage Coast Ranger.

Cleveland Way

Alan Staniforth

Aurum
Press

in association with

Walk
UNLIMITED

Brimming with creative inspiration, how-to projects and useful information to enrich your everyday life, Quarto Knows is a favourite destination for those pursuing their interests and passions. Visit our site and dig deeper with our books into your area of interest: Quarto Creates, Quarto Cooks, Quarto Homes, Quarto Lives, Quarto Drives, Quarto Explores, Quarto Gifts, or Quarto Kids.

For Richard Bell and Ian Sampson who generously shared their deep knowledge of the North York Moors.

The author wishes to acknowledge the help and patience of his wife, Pat, and the National Trail Officer, Malcolm Hodgson, in the compilation of this volume.

This revised and updated edition first published in 2019 by Aurum Press, an imprint of The Quarto Group
The Old Brewery, 6 Blundell Street, London N7 9BH, United Kingdom
www.QuartoKnows.com
in association with Walk Unlimited
www.walk.co.uk • www.nationaltrail.co.uk

© 2019 Quarto Publishing plc.

Images © 2012 by Natural England, except pages 15, 19, 24, 39, 57, 84-5, 97, 101, 104-5, 106, 108-9 © 2012 Mike Kipling; pages 115, 131 © 2012 Corbis; pages 1, 2-3, 12-13, 20-21, 27, 62, 73, 76, 82, 90, 122, 133, 134-5 © 2012 Alamy; 44-45, 49, 58-59, 95, 116-117, 128 © Alamy 2019.

This product includes mapping data licensed from Ordnance Survey® with the permission of the Controller of Her Majesty's Stationery Office. © Crown copyright 2013. All rights reserved. Licence number 43453U. Ordnance Survey and Travelmaster are registered trademarks and the Ordnance Survey symbol and Explorer are trademarks of Ordnance Survey, the national mapping agency of Great Britain.

All rights reserved. No part of this book may be reproduced or utilised in any form or by any means, electronic or mechanical, including photocopying, recording or by any information storage and retrieval system, without permission in writing from Aurum Press.

Every effort has been made to trace the copyright holders of material quoted in this book. If application is made in writing to the publisher, any omissions will be included in future editions.

A catalogue record for this book is available from the British Library.

ISBN 978 1 78131 503 3

Design by Rosamund Bird

Printed and bound by CPI Group (UK) Ltd, Croydon, CR0 4YY

Cover: *Cleveland Way, flanked by heather, on Busby Moor*
Half-title page: *Fishing boat at Runswick Bay*
Title page: *River Esk, Whitby*

Aurum Press want to ensure that these National Trail Guides are always as up to date as possible – but stiles collapse, pubs close and bus services change all the time. If, on walking this path, you discover any important changes that future walkers need to be aware of, do let us know. Either email us on **trailguides@quarto.com** with your comments, or, if you take the trouble to drop us a line to:

Trail Guides, Aurum Press, 74–77 White Lion Street, London N1 9PF,

we'll send you a free guide of your choice as thanks.

Contents

How to use this guide

This guide to the 109 mile (175km) Cleveland Way National Trail is in three parts:

- The introduction, with a background to the walk and the region and advice for those walking the route.

- A detailed description of the route, divided into ten sections, each with its appropriate maps. The total length for each section includes the distance walked through towns and villages. This part of the guide also includes information on places and topics of interest en route. These are numbered consecutively both on the maps and within the text.

- The last part of the guide includes useful information covering local transport, accommodation and equipment.

The maps have been prepared for this Trail Guide by the Ordnance Survey using the 1:25 000 Explorer or Outdoor Leisure map as a base. The line of the Cleveland Way is shown in yellow, with the status of the Trail – footpath or bridleway, for example – shown in green underneath. Walkers are reminded that virtually all the land over which the Way passes is privately owned; please do not stray from the path. The route is clearly signposted 'Cleveland Way' and these signs are frequently supplemented with the distinctive acorn symbol used for all National Trails. Bold letters on the maps and in the text indicate important points to look out for while walking. Should any part of the Cleveland Way need to be diverted for maintenance work or for other reasons, the alternative route will be clearly marked on the ground.

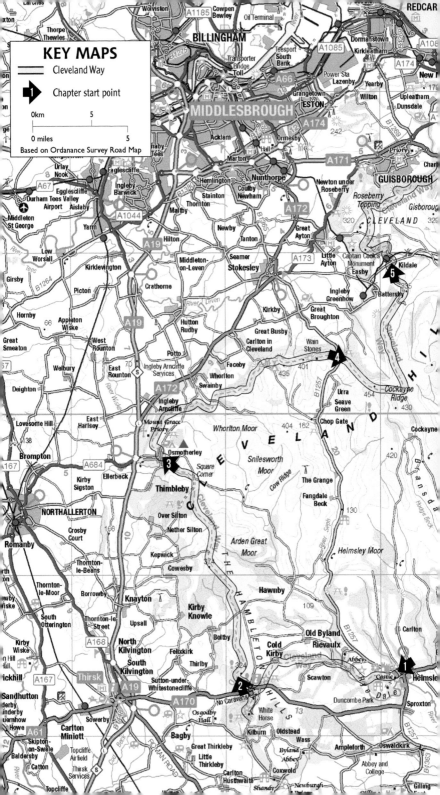

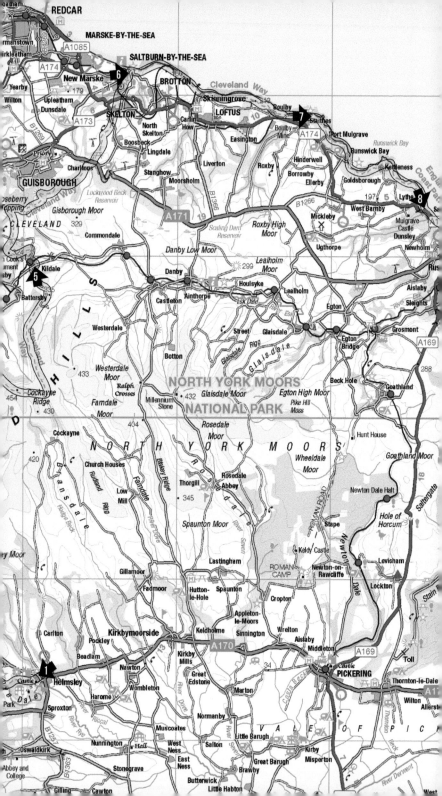

KEY MAPS

Cleveland Way

Chapter start point

0km 5

0 miles 5

Based on Ordanance Survey Road Map

WHITBY

Saltwick Bay

Cleveland Way

Stainsacre

Hawsker

B1447

Raw

rpe

Ness Point or
North Cheek

Robin Hood's Bay

Fylingthorpe

9

Robin Hood's Bay

Old Peak or
South Cheek

A171

Ravenscar

gdales Moor

n Howe

Rigg

18

Staintondale

England Coast Path

Harwood Dale

Cloughton
Newlands

Cloughton Wyke

Cloughton

A171

Silpho

Burniston

A165

Cromer Point

Langdale
End

Broxa

200

Suffield

Scalby

Scalby
Mills

Scalby Ness Rocks

Hackness

Everley

Castle

SCARBOROUGH

A170

10

Black Rocks

East Ayton

West Ayton

Hutton
Buscel

Irton

Osgodby

Cayton
Bay

Cleveland Way

Sawdon

Seamer

Eastfield

A165

The Wyke

Snainton

Wykeham

A64

Cayton

A1039

Brompton

C
a
s

River Hertford

Lebberston

Gristhorpe

FILEY

Staxton
Services

Flixton

Folkton

A1039

Filey Bay

Willerby

Muston

Primrose Valley Holiday Village

Staxton

Yorkshire Wolds

Hunmanby

Reighton Sands Holiday Village

Sherburn

Ganton

Distance checklist

This list will assist you in calculating the distances between places where you may be planning to stay overnight, or in checking your progress along the way.

	approx. distance from previous location	
	miles	km
Helmsley	0	0
Rievaulx Bridge	2.8	4.5
Cold Kirby	2.9	4.7
White Horse	3.1	5.0
Sutton Bank	1.4	2.3
Sneck Yate	2.4	5.5
Black Hambleton	5.2	8.4
Osmotherley	2.8	4.5
Scarth Nick	2.9	4.7
Carlton Bank	4.3	6.9
Clay Bank	3.9	6.3
Bloworth Crossing	3.2	5.1
Kildale	6.0	9.7
Roseberry Topping	4.3	6.9
Slapewath	6.0	9.7
Skelton	2.5	4.0
Saltburn	1.9	3.1
Skinningrove	2.9	6.3
Staithes	4.9	7.9
Runswick	3.4	5.5
Sandsend	5.1	8.2
Whitby	3.1	5.0
Robin Hood's Bay	7.0	11.3
Ravenscar	3.4	5.5
Scarborough (Corner) (North Bay)	10.2	16.4
Scarborough (Spa)	2.3	3.7
Cayton Bay	2.9	4.7
Filey Brigg	4.4	7.1

Preface

The beauty of walking the Cleveland Way lies in the great variety of landscapes through which you pass – you'll discover just why much of the Way lies within a National Park and a Heritage Coast. Attractive farmland, woods and heather moorland dominate the first half of the walk while dramatic cliffs, secluded coves and sandy beaches are your companions from Saltburn to Filey. Scattered throughout this ever changing vista you will find charming villages and historic edifices such as Helmsley Castle and Whitby Abbey, as well as the often more subtle remains left by ancient man. The effect of man's hand on the countryside will also be visible in bygone workings for once valuable minerals. The weather, whatever you encounter, will add another dimension to your experience while the North Sea will never appear the same from one day to the next.

The Cleveland Way is funded and promoted by Natural England and is liberally waymarked by signposts and the distinctive acorn symbol, a sign of quality used exclusively on the National Trails of England and Wales.

However you choose to walk the Way, this guide will keep you on the right track and provide useful, interesting and, hopefully, entertaining information to enhance your walk. Enjoy!

The Victorian White Horse at Kilburn, which is best viewed from a distance.

The former fishing village of Staithes has great character and close links with the explorer Captain Cook.

PART ONE
Introduction

Introduction

The landscapes of the 109 mile (175km) Cleveland Way range from high heather clad moorland to sheer coastal cliffs, from rolling farmland to steep inland escarpments, from sandy beaches to attractive woodland. Spread throughout these landscapes are ancient burial mounds, stone crosses, old routeways and relics of ancient industries. You will also see attractive villages and small towns with the occasional historic castle and abbey. In short, the Cleveland Way offers a variety of scenery rarely seen on any of the other National Trails throughout the country. Beginning in the old market town of Helmsley, the Way traces a horseshoe route around three sides of the North York Moors National Park, designated in 1952 for its magnificent scenery and wildlife. Following the path along the high western escarpment there are superb distant views over the Vale of Mowbray to the far hills of the Yorkshire Dales National Park. Further north the views extend across the valley of the River Tees to County Durham and beyond. For nearly half its length you follow the dramatic coastline from Saltburn to Filey, much of which forms the North Yorkshire and Cleveland Heritage Coast. Defined in 1974, this is one of a number of coastlines around England which are given special protection and where particular efforts are made for people to enjoy the area. The Way follows the undulating path clinging close to the cliff top and occasionally descending to the shore. The Cleveland Way has much to offer; take your time and savour its delights.

Hasty Bank is renowned for its outstanding views, on one side across to Teesside, on the other into the Bilsdale Valley.

Welcome to the Cleveland Way

The first National Trail to be established in England was the 268 mile (431km) Pennine Way, following a route along the backbone of England from the Peak District to Northumberland. It was

only four years later that the second trail, the Cleveland Way, was opened at Helmsley Castle in May 1969. The chosen route was a 'natural', following distinct escarpments and sea cliffs for 109 miles (175km) between Helmsley and Filey. Originally referred to as the 'Moors and Coast Path' the name Cleveland Way soon took precedence and the definitive white acorn symbol began to appear as a route marker. Fifty years ago public footpaths and bridleways were not as well maintained as they are today and there was no 'Open Access'. Today, there are a huge number of long distance walks including a total of fifteen National Trails throughout England. The creation of a continuous coastal path around the whole of England includes the coast section of the Cleveland Way. Look out for the England Coast Path signs as you walk from Saltburn to Filey.

The Way is managed by a partnership, established in 1989, of the North York Moors National Park Authority, Scarborough Borough Council, Redcar and Cleveland Borough Council together with Natural England. The Project works to maintain a high quality route for walkers and also liaises with local businesses to provide services required during a walk. Protecting the landscape and wildlife along the route is a top priority and with high numbers of users, maintenance of the path surface has become increasingly important. Many miles of old sandstone slabs have been laid over softer ground to protect the heather moorland. Traditional techniques of stone pitching are used on steeper ground while limestone aggregate makes a good walking surface around Sutton Bank and elsewhere. Natural erosion plus a heavy footfall in some locations along the coast has led to cliff falls, necessitating moving the path back to provide a safe walking corridor. The replacement of dozens of stiles with hand gates, particularly along popular sections of the route used by local people, has opened much of the route for the less agile walker.

Our National Park

A common misconception about England's National Parks is that they are owned by the nation. England has a history of private land ownership dating back to the Norman Conquest so when, in the 1950s, our first National Parks were established, the term 'national' was used in the sense of 'national importance' rather than 'nationally owned'. The North York Moors National Park covers over 500 sq miles (1295 sq km), most of it still owned privately, and contains the largest area of heather moorland in England. There are over 1,400 miles (2,250km) of public paths and bridleways plus huge areas of 'Open Access' land. This comes with responsibilities and certain restrictions. Please see the inside of the back cover of this guide for further information.

The Rocks Beneath

The North York Moors form a largely upland area with distinct physical boundaries, the Cleveland Hills to the west, the cliffs overlooking the North Sea to the east and the dip slope of

the Tabular Hills to the south. Most of the rocks forming this block were laid down as sediments in ancient seas and river deltas up to 200 million years ago during Jurassic times. Uplifted and eroded in later times they now form the landscape we enjoy today. The weathering of the sandstones of the high moors produce a thin acidic soil suiting heather, which has become the principle species. Streams cutting into this high plateau have exposed shales in the valley bottoms which gives rise to a somewhat better soil, while the limestones of the southern slopes produce thin but rich soils.

At Gribdale Gate, between Captain Cook's Monument and Roseberry Topping, you cross the Cleveland Dyke. Easily missed, this once molten lava was forced into the rocks of the moors some 57 million years ago and is the only example of volcanic activity in the area. In more recent geological times, the last glaciation left its mark on the landscape in the form of clays and sands which today plaster some of the older rocks of the area, particularly along the coastline. The whole region is famous for its structural geology and range of fossils, all described in the unique Rotunda Museum in Scarborough, which is well worth a deviation if you can spare the time.

Animals and Plants

An old name for the North York Moors is 'Black-a-moor'. For some of the year the moors are indeed black and sombre, but visit in summer and you'll enjoy the largest carpet of purple heather in England. The Scotch Heather or Ling is the most common of several heath species and produces millions of tiny purple flowers. Pollen rises in clouds as you walk through the heather and the scent can be intoxicating. This is also home to the red grouse, a game bird that can be seen on the moor at any time of the year. In spring the curlew returns from the coast to nest, along with the lapwing, snipe and golden plover. You may also be lucky enough to see a merlin, Britain's smallest bird of prey. The woodlands and field edges burst into life in spring with a range of colour and bird song.

Along the coastal section of the Way you may meet scurvy grass, a low white flower with fleshy leaves, once eaten to prevent scurvy. A tall, greenish yellow plant also common on the coast is alexanders, all parts of which are edible when properly prepared. The coast is also a rich area for bird watching or for rummaging in rock pools and at Ravenscar there is a good chance of seeing seals off the headland.

The Use of the Land

One of the glories of the North York Moors is its vast expanse of heather moorland. And yet this apparently natural landscape is in fact 'man made'. The natural woodland cover which evolved following the end of the last Ice Age was gradually destroyed by early man and heather moorland took its place. Today this habitat is maintained as a result of the management of the land as grouse moor. Left to its own devices much of the moor would revert to woodland.

Moving from the high moors, early man settled in the dales and around the fringes of the upland and so began a pattern of farming that continues to this day. The Cistercian monks of Rievaulx and elsewhere are credited with introducing intensive sheep farming to the area; flocks still graze the high moor while less hardy breeds stock the lower pastures. Arable farming occupies large parts of the southern limestone fringe. Following the First World War vast conifer plantations were established, particularly in the south east of the area. In a more enlightened era these 'dark serried ranks' are gradually being felled and replanted in a more attractive manner. The moors have attracted visitors over many decades but today the use of the land for recreation has become a mainstay of the local economy.

The red grouse is an iconic bird, sure to be spotted on the heather moorland of the North York Moors National Park.

Black Nab, Saltwick Bay

Ancient Days

Before the arrival of men from the continent most of Britain was clad in forest, but since those early arrivals the pace of change has escalated. Walking the Cleveland Way you pass by evidence from nearly all the major periods of English history. Stone Age relics are scant but Bronze Age evidence is common. There are the remains of Iron Age forts, Roman signal stations and Norman castles, ancient cottages and grand houses. Old industry has left its mark and the landscape itself tells of centuries of change. Even when the National Park was designated in 1952 the area was a bit 'out on a limb'. Tourists were heading for the Lake District, Yorkshire Dales or Scotland. Slowly, however, the secrets of the moors were disclosed and visitors started heading east. Modern times had arrived. The changes which have brought about the beauty and interest we enjoy in the moors today continue. Change is inevitable, but with the protection which national park status endows the area will continue to remain beautiful for centuries to come.

Planning your Walk

A few people have been known to run the Cleveland Way in a day. . . what a waste! In planning your walk allow time to appreciate your surroundings, watch wildlife, deviate a little off course and time to sit and admire. *'A poor life this if, full of care, We have no time to stand and stare'* (W. H. Davies). The route covers 109 miles (175km) so eight to ten days would allow a leisurely walk. Where to stop and start each day will depend to some extent on your fitness, speed of walking and accommodation en route. Parts of the route are quite strenuous, particularly along the escarpment of the Cleveland Hills and there are also some steep climbs along the coastal section. An average walking pace of around 2 miles per hour

(3.2km) is a good general guide, but allow for those steep climbs.

Following the Way

The Cleveland Way is so well signed that it would be difficult to stray from the route. Signs can be lost or damaged, however, so reference to maps is sometimes essential. Frequent signposts routed with the words 'Cleveland Way' will be seen at all major path junctions and roads, while the acorn symbol on gateposts or walls gives confirmation of the correct route. When following the coast, keep the sea on your left!

Watch the Weather

Weather in the North York Moors arrives mainly from two directions, west and north east. The westerly wind can be pretty cool, particularly when walking along the western escarpment; it can also be wet as it drives in over the Pennines. The north easterlies are usually even cooler when you're exposed along the coastal cliffs, and you may be unfortunate enough to occasionally encounter a damp coast fog or 'sea fret' which sometimes clings to the coastline. Now for the good news! The east side of England is a lot drier than the west and when the sun shines there is no better place to be.

Safety First

Remember, your safety is your responsibility. If you have planned your walk well, are carrying the right equipment and use your common sense there should be no problems. However, accidents do happen. Take particular care in windy weather while walking the high hills and coast path. Know where your escape routes are in the event of bad visibility or accidents. Mobile phone reception on the moors can be patchy so don't rely on it. In the unlikely event of serious problems, dial 112 or contact the police, 999, who will call out the local Mountain Rescue Team.

The western escarpment looks across the Hambleton Hills to Boltby Forest.

Ivy Scar on Sutton Bank – just one of the spectacular views along the Cleveland Way.

PART TWO
Cleveland Way

Helmsley to Sutton Bank

10 miles (16.1km)
past Rievaulx and the White Horse of Kilburn

Ascent 1,888 feet (575 metres)
Lowest point Helmsley 188 feet (57 metres)
Highest point Casten Dyke, near Sutton Bank 965 feet (294 metres)

Woodland, valleys and the gently rising limestone slopes of the Hambleton Hills set the scene for this first section of the Cleveland Way. Culminating in the dramatic escarpment at Sutton Bank, overlooking the Vales of York and Mowbray, this is a gentle introduction to the varied terrain ahead. There are some fine views to enjoy, so don't forget to look back occasionally. Helmsley Castle and Rievaulx Abbey are the two most dominant buildings but lesser structures like Griff Lodge and Rievaulx Bridge are also worth a pause. Whatever the season, the flora and fauna is varied and colourful with perhaps a chance to glimpse a buzzard or an adder, or to enjoy the wide range of flowers in wood or hedgerow.

However you travel to Helmsley, you are sure to end up in the Market Square **1** where the Cleveland Way begins at the dominating Feversham Memorial in the middle of the square **A**. The Town Hall is another impressive structure with its red tile roof and striking white lantern. Walk down the left hand side of this building to Bridge Street. Cross the road on a slight diagonal to the right and walk up the broad path towards Helmsley Castle **2**. This is the most impressive approach to the castle which is worth a closer look if you can spare the time. At

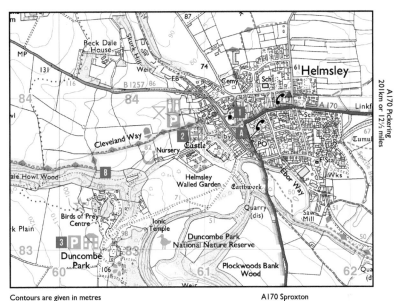

Contours are given in metres
The vertical interval is 10m

A170 Sproxton
1km or ½ mile

A170 Pickering
20km or 12½ miles

Helmsley to Sutton Bank

The gaunt ruins of Helmsley Castle, besieged by Parliamentary troops during the Civil War in 1644.

the castle entrance turn right towards the car park and then diagonally across the park to the large sculpted Cleveland Way stone. You will find a similar stone to this when your reach journey's end at Filey.

Follow the broad track which climbs gradually up the dip slope of the Hambleton Hills to a point where the path turns sharp left towards the wood. Pause to look back towards the castle and the walled garden of Duncombe Park **3**.

Turn right alongside the wood **B** and bear left to drop down steps into a small dry valley. Continue up the other side and ahead to a small attractive stone building. This is Griff Lodge, an old gateway into Duncombe Park which takes its name from the remains of a mediaeval village on the hilltop above Rievaulx. The name Griff is, however, much older, first recorded in

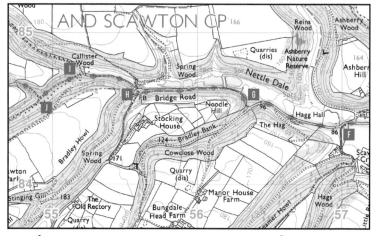

AND SCAWTON CP ·166

Reins Wood

Ashberry Wood

Callister Wood

Quarries (dis)

Ashberry Nature Reserve

164

Ashberr Hill

Spring Wood

Nettle Dale

Grass Keld

FB   Bridge Road

Noodle Hill

96

Hagg Hall

Stocking House

Bradley Bank

The Hag

86

Bradley Howl

124

Cowclose Wood

Sca Cr

Spring Wood   171

Quarry (dis)

090

wton ark

84

Stinging Gill   183   The Old Rectory

Manor House Farm

Hags Wood

55   Quarry

Bungdale Head Farm   56

180

57

Contours are given in metres
The vertical interval is 10m

Picturesque Helmsley makes a delightful start to the Cleveland Way.

the Domesday Book of 1086. Follow the broad track **C** with the lodge on your right and gradually descend through the woodland, passing an old limestone quarry before reaching the road where you turn left **D**.

You now have a little road walking to contend with, but keep a lookout on the right for distant views of Rievaulx Abbey, **4** a magnificent Cistercian ruin dating from 1132 and set in a beautiful valley on the banks of the River Rye.

When you reach the road junction **E** you could make a detour to the right to visit the abbey but this will add another mile (1.6km) to your walk plus time to look around.

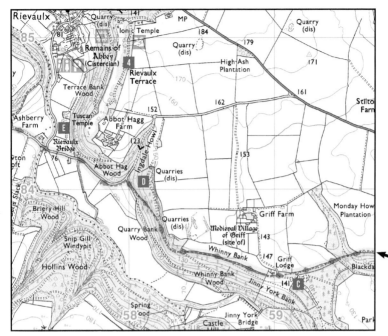

Contours are given in metres
The vertical interval is 10m

The Way now crosses Rievaulx Bridge, an ancient high arched stone bridge which was rebuilt following severe flooding which destroyed the earlier structure in 1754. Continue along the tarmac road, keeping left at the next junction **F** on the Thirsk/Scawton road.

Continue along the road for another half mile (0.8km) and near the bend turn right **G** into Nettle Dale along a broad limestone track past the fishing lakes on your right. These lakes have been created as wildlife and fishing lakes and are fed from springs in the nearby appropriately named Spring Wood.

Where the track bends to the left **H**, turn right over the stepping stones. The stream here is typical of a limestone area with exceptionally clear water. Once through the gate you continue

along a broad track and at the junction bear left **I** up Flassen Dale. This is another typical dry valley, the stream that once carved it having disappeared underground long ago.

A prominent barbecue site a short way up the valley is your guide to a right turn **J** up a short tributary valley which brings you up onto the dip slope again and a long straight rough stone lane, Low Field Lane.

Over to your right in the distance you may see the mast of the Bilsdale broadcasting and telecommunications transmitting station. Standing on the 1247 feet (380m) contour, the mast itself is over 1000 feet (305m) high and, weather permitting, can be seen from many locations along the Cleveland Way.

Approaching Cold Kirby the church comes into view and just past the farm buildings turn right off the track and drop down a path into a small wood **K**. Continue up the opposite side where in late summer you may be hit by the strong aniseed scent of sweet cicely, which grows here in profusion. Emerge onto the road at Cold Kirby, appropriately named if there happens to be a good easterly wind blowing. Go straight ahead up through the village and past the last house on the left, then turn left **L** along a farm track.

The trail bends to the right and then turns left. Look back for good views to the Yorkshire Wolds and the Howardian Hills. Continue ahead through a gate and head towards the conifer woods where you turn right **M**. Pass the horse racing stables and at the rough tarmac road turn left **N** and follow this to the A170. The large building by the roadside was once the Hambleton Inn, one of the principal inns on the old drove road but sadly, like so many others, it is now closed.

Turn right along the main road until you reach a left hand junction **O** which leads to the Yorkshire Gliding Club. Your path now enters the forest following a 45 degree angle between the two roads. On your right is a prominent ridge and ditch known as the

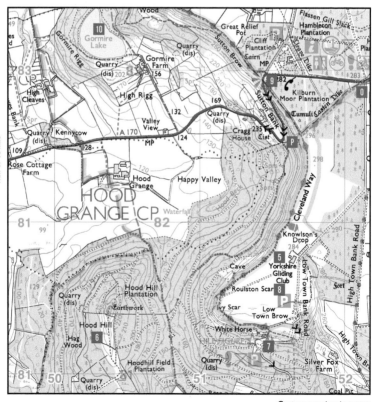

Contours are given in metres
The vertical interval is 10m

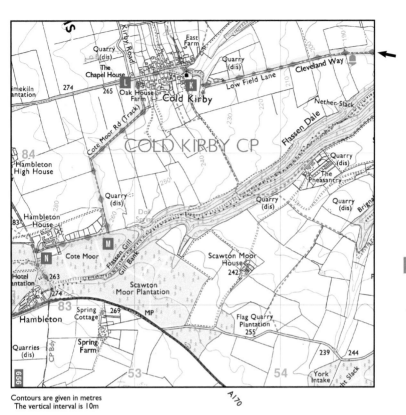

Contours are given in metres
The vertical interval is 10m

Casten Dyke, one of many prehistoric boundaries in this area.

You will suddenly emerge from the trees onto the edge of the Hambleton escarpment **P** with the land falling dramatically away below you for over 650 feet (200m). Turn left on a good limestone path and follow the edge of the escarpment, with the gliding club airfield and clubhouse on your left **5**. Watch out for low flying gliders as they are hauled up into the heavens. From here there are impressive views towards the Pennine hills and down the Vale of York. On a clear day you will be able to pick out the towers of York Minster and at least two power stations. Roulston Scar and the area now occupied by the

gliding club was once the site of a huge Iron Age fort **8**, one of the largest in the country, dating from around 400BC.

The almost conical Hood Hill **6** stands out from the scarp edge while Lake Gormire **10** can be seen down to the right – a remnant of our glacial heritage. The path swings to the left to gain the top of the White Horse of Kilburn **7**, best seen from a distance – you are currently standing on the horse's back.

Retrace your steps along the escarpment and cross the A170 at Sutton Bank where you will find the National Park Information Centre **9**, toilets and refreshments and the end of this first section of your walk.

Helmsley Market

If you happen to arrive in Helmsley on a Friday you can enjoy visiting the busy market **1** with its colourful awnings and merchandise ranging from fruit and veg to fish and fowl, leather products, fancy goods, home-made items and much more. But imagine you are standing here in the 18th century. The ground is compounded earth, transformed into 'slush and muck' in wet weather. Many of the buildings you see today do not exist and those that do are mainly low and thatched. The castle keep still dominates the scene and over in the far corner a smaller and simpler church predates the present All Saints' Church. The black and white half-timbered building on the north side of the square will eventually be incorporated into the Black Swan Hotel. Baron Feversham's memorial doesn't exist yet but the market cross is still the focal point of the market which, unlike today, is dominated by livestock sales. Come back to the present and enjoy a coffee in one of the town's many cafes before striding out to Filey.

Memorial to an Earl

Fresh from his success in designing the Albert Memorial in London in 1863, George Gilbert Scott (later Sir George) set to work at the request of the new Earl of Feversham to create a memorial **A** to his late father, the 2nd Baron Feversham who had died in 1867. Similarities between the two memorials are obvious, although the memorial in Helmsley has suffered rather more from the ravages of time. The statue of the Baron in his full regalia was sculpted

by Matthew Noble, a Yorkshire sculptor born at Hackness near Scarborough.

A Stately Home

Tucked away in a corner of Helmsley is the entrance to Duncombe Park **3**, a 450 acre (182 hectare) estate of rolling parkland, gardens and ancient woodland within which stands the house of the same name. The building occupies a commanding position close to an escarpment overlooking the valley of the River Rye. William Wakefield, a close friend of the famous architect Vanbrugh, commenced building in 1713 and the work was completed by c.1730. This impressive early Georgian structure, to which wings were added at a later date, was badly damaged by fire 1879 and again in 1895. After rebuilding it was leased, in 1925, to the Woodard Trust and opened as a girls' boarding school. In 1985 it reverted to a private residence. Over 255 acres (103 hectares) of the estate were designated a National Nature Reserve in 1994 in order to protect some of the oldest and tallest trees in the north of England. These reflect the woodland which once existed over large parts of the country and provides a home for a wide range of wood-feeding insects and fungi, many of them rare in Britain.

A Commanding Castle

The start of the Cleveland Way in Helmsley is arguably the most impressive of all the National Trails. As you leave the Market Place the 100 foot (30m) high edifice of Helmsley Castle **2** rears above you. Following the Norman Conquest in 1066 William granted the land around

The early Georgian mansion at Duncombe Park was designed by William Wakefield, friend of the famous architect Vanbrugh.

PARKLAND

RIVER & COUNTRY WALKS

Helmsley to his half-brother Robert de Mortain. The date for the raising of the first castle, which would probably have been constructed in wood, is uncertain. Some of the present earthworks, however, date from this period and were utilized by later owners of the castle for the basis of their stone built structure. Walter l'Espec, founder of Rievaulx Abbey, was probably the first to erect a stone building on the site, but the oldest stonework visible today dates from the end of the 12th century in the time of Robert de Ros. Additions over succeeding centuries have extended and strengthened the original buildings, although it seems that the castle's only military experience was a three month siege in 1644, after which it was virtually abandoned.

Splendid Rievaulx

The Cistercian, or white monks as they were known because they wore a white habit, certainly knew how to build. They also knew where to find an ideal location for a monastery **4**. The Cistercian Order was founded in France in 1098 as a reaction to what was seen as the slipping standards of the Benedictine Order. The Cistercians chose a life of absolute simplicity, denying themselves any luxury or wealth, accepting no gifts or tithes and having the most simple church furniture. Ceremonial was kept to a minimum with no litanies and little chanting. They were the Puritans of their day, observing strict rules and detaching themselves from the world. Theirs was to be a life dedicated to private prayer and study of the scriptures, cut off from all worldly distractions. And yet the Order quickly developed into one of the richest and most powerful in the country with huge business interests in sheep farming, iron working, fisheries and salt pans. So what changed?

Following the Norman Conquest of England in 1066 William gave extensive tracts of land to his supporters, among them Walter L'Espec, who became Lord of Helmsley. He in turn granted land in 1131 to a small group of

Cistercian monks who were seeking a remote and wild location 'away from the eyes of the world' to establish their simple church. Arriving in 1132 they soon realised that in order to devote their time entirely to meditation and contemplation they needed support for the daily essentials of life. Their solution was the establishment of a 'lower' order of lay brothers who spent only a brief time in religious observance. Within only a few decades the numbers of monks had risen to 150 and the lay brothers to nearly 500. In order to pay for the upkeep of this community and

The valley of the River Rye with the ruins of Rievaulx Abbey.

the labour required for the extensive building work on the abbey, the brothers developed granges or sheep farms in the outlying area with flocks numbering over fourteen thousand sheep, the wool from which was eagerly sought after by merchants from abroad. The monks also exploited the iron found in the surrounding hills and opened bloomeries to smelt the raw material. Other mining interests were established as far afield as West Yorkshire. Fisheries and salt works were set up on the banks of the River Tees.

The building work progressed rapidly, but due to the narrow nature of the valley the abbey had to be built not in the conventional east-west alignment but on a north-south plan. Canals, the remains of which can still be seen close to the abbey, were cut in order to bring building stone from quarries higher up the valley.

Undoubtedly the most famous abbot of Rievaulx was St Aelred who officiated as third abbot from 1147 until his death in 1167. He was well known throughout the western world for

A pastoral scene of great tranquillity in the Rye Valley near Rievaulx.

his sanctity and learning and was a respected friend of King Henry II. An often quoted line from St Aelred, *'Everywhere peace, everywhere serenity, and a marvellous freedom from the tumult of the world'* beautifully captures the tranquillity of Rievaulx's setting and the ideals of the first Cistercian monks.

However, by the early 1300s, Rievaulx's power and grandeur days were in decline. The extensive building works led to debt which resulted in the Crown bailing out the abbey on more than one occasion. Further trouble occurred in 1322 when the English, under Edward II, were roundly defeated at the nearby Battle of Old Byland. Edward is reported to have been at dinner at Rievaulx when he heard of the defeat and quickly fled, leaving behind the royal treasure which was seized by the Scots, who also sacked the abbey and made off with its *'books, chalices and the sacred ornaments.'* In 1348 the Black Death decimated populations throughout the country and Rievaulx

did not escape unscathed, the number of monks and lay brothers dropping dramatically. The final ignominy came with the Dissolution of the Monasteries in the 16th century. Henry VIII, with an eye on the monastic riches and only too aware of their allegiance to Rome, approved the passing of the First Suppression Act of 1534. Over the coming years some nine hundred religious houses throughout the country were closed. In 1538 Rievaulx was stripped of its remaining treasures and its lead roof and as the last twenty one monks and their abbot departed, the building was left to decay and serve as a source of local building stone. The glory of Rievaulx was over.

Revolx Bredg

"October 28th 1754 – A great and trable flud of water came by the rever Reye to Helmslay blakeymour, which came with such veamancy that it drove down to the ground 8 houses, 5 dwelling houses...It drove down most

parts of Helmsla Bredg and Revolx Bredg down to the ground" (From an eye witness account of the great Rye flood of 1754).

Revolx Bredg or, as we now call it, Rievaulx Bridge **E**, straddles the River Rye down stream from Rievaulx Abbey. The present stone humpbacked bridge was built following the destruction of the former bridge during the great flood in 1754 as described above. This earlier bridge was probably constructed by the lay brothers from Rievaulx soon after they established the abbey.

Free as a Bird!

The light aircraft, tow rope attached to your glider, trundles across the bumpy turf of the 320 foot (284m) high plateau forming the extreme south west corner of the North York Moors. Gathering speed the bumpiness suddenly ceases as you become airborne and then in a moment your stomach drops as you speed over the heads of the Cleveland Way walkers beneath and shoot out over the Vale of Mowbray hundreds of feet below. Climbing higher to find favourable uplifting air currents the tow rope is

Sutton Bank provides an ideal location for gliding.

eventually released as the light plane banks away to return to the airfield. You're on your own with only the rush of wind and fantastic views for company. It is the prevailing westerly winds and the shape of the land that make this such an ideal place for gliding. On a good day many gliders fill the air and may stay aloft for hours reaching incredible heights before gracefully descending to earth and a bumpy landing on the airfield. The Yorkshire Gliding Club **5** was established in 1934 and welcomes visitors to its cafe or to enjoy a flight with one of its instructors, an unforgettable experience.

An Ancient Volcano?

Standing on Roulston Scar looking across to the isolated peak of Hood Hill **6** it doesn't take much imagination to presume that you are looking at the remains of an extinct volcano. Sadly, this is not the case. Hood Hill is one of several outliers to be seen around the periphery of the North York Moors. All are features of erosion as over

Distinctive Hood Hill stands isolated from the Tabular Hills escarpment.

millennia softer rocks in the vicinity have been gradually worn away, leaving the harder core as striking features of the landscape. In the case of Hood Hill much of the erosion took place during the glacial period some ten to twenty thousand years ago, when ice blocked the whole of the Vale of York and meltwater coursed southwards between the edge of the escarpment and the ice, cutting off the hill from the adjacent scarp. Earthworks on the top of the hill suggest that it may once have been the site of a castle but although as a defensive site it has its merits, the lack of water would have been a serious setback in the event of an siege.

A White Horse at Kilburn

Travel north on a train from London and on a clear day the White Horse of Kilburn **7** makes a striking landmark on the distant slopes of the North York Moors. Travellers in the south of England may be familiar with figures of horses, people and even birds and military badges cut into the turf of the chalk downlands. While some of these are of modern vintage, others are thought to date back to prehistoric times. The Kilburn White Horse is the only such figure in the north of England and dates back to 1857. A massive 314 feet (96m) from head to tail, 228 feet (70m) tall and with a grass eye that can accommodate twenty standing adults, the figure is cut into a very steep slope on the hillside overlooking the picturesque village of Kilburn, also famous as the home of the woodcarver known as the Mouse Man of Kilburn. It is said that a local man, Thomas Taylor, having travelled in the south of England, suggested the creation of the horse above his home village. It was then left to the local schoolmaster, John Hodgson, to draw up a plan, stake out the outline and encourage a team of over thirty volunteers to cut away the turf to reveal the rock beneath. Geology, however, was not either Taylor or Hodgson's strong point. While figures in the south are cut into turf overlying chalk or white limestone, Kilburn's horse was revealed as a dirty grey when first exposed. Not to be thwarted, the locals spread tons of lime on the outline to create a white mare. Over the years the horse has required periodic grooming, chalk chippings being brought in from the nearby Yorkshire Wolds and spread over the outline. The horse is such a conspicuous landmark that during the Second World War it was covered up to prevent enemy aircraft pilots from recognising their position. Although the Cleveland Way arrives on the back of the horse, a far better view can be seen from Kilburn village or even from the tower of York Minster some 20 miles (32km) to the south west.

Iron Age Dykes & Hill Forts

One could say that the gentle slopes of the Hambleton Hills which end in the dramatic scarp overlooking the Vales of York and Mowbray are littered with prehistoric remains. These are not, however, imposing monuments such as Stonehenge, but offer more subtle evidence in the form of ditches, embankments, hollows and mounds. A keen eye is required to pick out these features, particularly when they are covered in vegetation during spring

and summer. Many of the remains date from the Iron Age around 400 BC, and while some were undoubtedly for defensive purposes, others were possibly boundaries between fields or tribal lands. Mystery still surrounds the true story.

Walking towards Sutton Bank along the Cleveland Way you will pass several lengths of ditch and parallel mounds, the Casten Dyke being particularly noticeable after passing the old Hambleton Inn on the A171. Although we can say with some certainty that these date from the Iron Age, mapping of their alignment has raised the question of whether these earthworks were modified as late as the 14th century during the Battle of Byland in 1322, when Scottish forces overwhelmed the English army of Edward II.

Evidence for the remains of an Iron Age hill fort on Roulston Scar **8** was first recorded in the 19th century, although due to a mapping error by the Ordnance Survey the information was 'lost' for some years. A section of the southern rampart was lost when the White Horse of Kilburn was cut in 1857. Excavations during the late 1960s and early 1970s revealed much more evidence for this huge fort which covered some 60 acres (c.24 hectares) and is the largest in the north of England. Further surveys and excavations were carried out in the early 21st century. We now know that at least parts of the fort were defended by a wooden palisade as well as a mound and ditch, which must have taken a huge amount of material and time to build. Many such forts were probably fortified settlements and may also have been built as a statement of power.

2 Sutton Bank to Osmotherley

11¼ miles (18km)
via Sneck Yat and Black Hambleton

Ascent 1,393 feet (425 metres)
Descent 1,775 feet (541 metres)
Lowest point Osmotherley 536 feet (163 metres)
Highest point Black Hambleton 1,269 feet (387 metres)

For most of this next length of the Cleveland Way the route follows the edge of the escarpment at around 1,000 feet (320m) above sea level and little direction is required. If the weather is good this is one of the finest walks in the country with fantastic views stretching for miles in any of three directions. Peer into the depths of Lake Gormire 600 feet (170m) below. Pick out the hills of the Yorkshire Dales over to the west and Roseberry Topping to the north. Watch out for red grouse and, if you are walking in August, enjoy the unique scent of the heather on Black Hambleton.

From the National Park Centre walk towards the escarpment with the A170 on your left, cross a minor road and take the limestone path which quickly takes you onto the escarpment and to 'The Finest View in England', that is, according to Alf White aka James Herriot. Some may dispute this but all must agree that it's a pretty good outlook.

You'll be sharing part of this route with cyclists as Sutton Bank is now a very popular off-road cycling venue with bikes for hire at the Sutton Bank Centre.

There are some fine examples of old larch tree here which with their twisted trunks and branches clearly demonstrate the effect of the westerly winds. The woodlands below Whitestone Cliff are more sheltered and a large part of them are protected as a nature reserve by the Yorkshire Wildlife Trust. Below is Lake Gormire **10**, one of the few natural lakes in Yorkshire and a remnant from our glacial history of thousands of years ago.

Avoid all of the several routes to the right which would take you over Hambleton Down and continue along the well-defined path above Whitestone Cliff and onward to Boltby Scar. A hill fort and settlement is marked on the OS map at this point but very little can be discerned today. There are, however, fissures in the ground where the limestone cliffs are slowly eroding; these are noted as Windypits on the map.

The appropriately named High Barn **A** is the next landmark on the route. Now derelict, it is surrounded by a shelterbelt of ancient sycamore trees.

Contours are given in metres
The vertical interval is 10m

*The Hambleton Drove Road,
once used by cattle drovers.*

Beyond here the route gradually drops to cross the road at Sneck Yate **B** and enters Boltby Forest. 'Yate' is a local word meaning 'gate' and the name is pronounced 'yat'.

The route now follows a pleasant gradually descending path through beech woods to join a minor road. You have a short, steep climb up the road, avoiding any offshoots until you reach High Paradise Farm. The tea room here is well worth a stop, not only for the tea and cake but also for the interesting interior and especially its eclectic collection of old books.

Go straight through the farm yard and where the track joins another at right angles **C**, turn left along the broad track which is part of the old road once used by Scottish drovers bringing cattle to markets in the south. By following the higher ground where possible, the drovers avoided having to pay tolls on the lower turnpike road. The high ground also offered the opportunity of free grazing for the cattle.

Continue ahead through conifer trees and then through a gate onto the open moor where you will see the base and broken shaft of Steeple Cross **12**, one of many moorland crosses. Some still act as marker stones for estate and civil boundaries.

A good stone track now continues ahead over heather moorland. This will be the first area of moorland you will have encountered on the walk, but it will not be the last. You may occasionally be startled by a dark brown bird exploding from the heather with a rapid call of 'go-back; go-back; go-back'. This is the red grouse, a native of the moors in residence throughout the year. Much of the moorland is managed as grouse moor to support shooting which commences on 'The Glorious Twelfth' i.e. 12th August.

The route is now fairly level for some distance and heather gives way to rough grassland before returning once again to heather moorland, a reflection of a change in the local geology.

A minor road climbs the escarpment coming to an end at a gateway on your left **D**. The road gives access to the moor for farmers and gamekeepers but also once serviced large limestone quarries below the scarp edge. Limestone was,

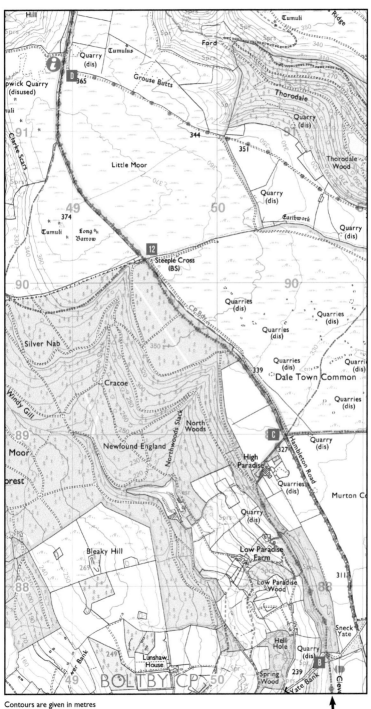

Contours are given in metres
The vertical interval is 10m

Hawnby
4km or 2½ miles

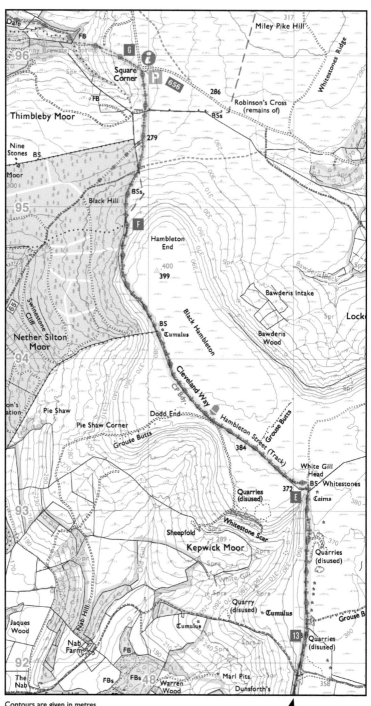

Contours are given in metres
The vertical interval is 10m

and still is, an important material used in the agricultural and construction industries, although its exploitation is now concentrated on several large quarries elsewhere. The hummocky ground here locates some of the smaller, long abandoned quarries **13**.

Strung out along the drove road were a number of inns where the drovers could rest their animals and service their own requirements. All four inns within the moors are now closed. Limekiln House, once situated near here, would have been used by the local quarry men as well as the drovers. Only a pile of rubble remains to mark its location.

The stone wall on your left is constructed from limestone and is built without mortar. As you walk further ahead you may notice that the same wall is now built of sandstone, another indication of the changing geology beneath your feet.

At White Gill Head **E**, just after crossing the cattle grid, bear left at the track junction. A gentle climb along the flank of Black Hambleton brings you to a viewpoint **F** looking towards your destination at Osmotherley.

Continue ahead downhill to where the track joins the road at Square Corner **G**. Veer diagonally left downhill on a steep but well paved path to Oakdale. At the

Swaledale is the traditional breed of sheep found on the heather moorland.

bottom, cross the footbridge which merges onto a broad track alongside the former reservoir. Pass Oakdale House on your right then continue over the bridge and up the hill to join the road **H**.

Turn left down the road for only a few yards, then sharp right up a track to reach White House Farm gate **I**. Although the obvious route should be through the gate, this is not the legal right of way. Walk a few yards past the gate and you will see a squeeze stile on the left.

Rejoin the farm track and just before the farm veer right to drop down into the woods. Cross the track, then the footbridge **J** over Cod Beck and climb steeply up the other side. Reaching the top you pass through a gate to follow the well-paved path between hedge and fence.

Pass through several more squeeze stiles, cross the lane and continue ahead between the houses to suddenly and surprisingly emerge in Osmotherley at the war memorial and opposite the market cross **14**.

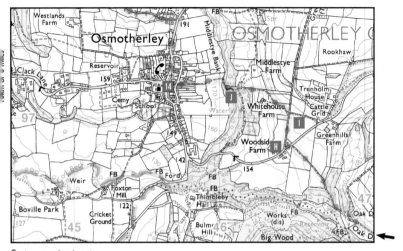

Contours are given in metres
The vertical interval is 10m

*Kepwick Quarry, showing
the disused incline tramway.*

The Vale of Mowbray and Lake Gormire from Sutton Bank.

Sutton Bank

'On a clear day you can see forever'. Well, perhaps not quite that far, but on a good day the views from Sutton Bank **9** are both extensive and impressive. Described by Alf Wight, alias James Herriot, as 'the finest view in England', the scene stretches northwards towards Cleveland and Durham, west to the Yorkshire Dales and south to York and beyond. Closer to hand is the 'bottomless' Gormire Lake, backed by the great Whitestone Cliff from which the distant village of Sutton-under-Whitestonecliffe takes its name. In a little over half a mile (0.8km) the A170 climbs over 360 feet (110m) at a maximum gradient of 1 in 4 (25 per cent) and includes several severe hairpin bends. In the early 20th century, when road traffic was far less than today, motor cycle trials were held on the bank. Although width and surface have improved over the years, the gradient is the same and still catches out unwary drivers. An HGV stuck on the bank is an all too frequent event, and can close the road for hours.

William Wordsworth, his sister Dorothy and his new bride Mary paused at the top of the bank in October 1802 on their way back to the Lake District following William and Mary's marriage at Brompton near Scarborough. What a different sight would fill their vision today. The National Park Information Centre with its shop, cafe and bike hire facility has evolved to cater for the thousands of tourists who pass this way en route for the moors and coast. Once a quiet backwater Sutton Bank is now a gateway to the National Park.

Bottomless Gormire!

Is Lake Gormire **10** bottomless? Springs at the foot of the escarpment continue to drain water into the lake but no stream is seen to leave it.

Conclusion? It must be bottomless. In reality of course, the water gradually seeps away into the rocks below.

Gormire is usually regarded as one of only four natural lakes to occur in Yorkshire, the others being Semmerwater and Malham Tarn in the Yorkshire Dales and Hornsea Mere in the East Riding. During the last great Ice Age, ice filled most of the Vale of York and impinged upon the cliffs at Sutton Bank. Towards the end of the Ice Age some ten to twenty thousand years ago, water from the melting ice coursed along between the cliff face and the edge of the ice, often cutting into the hillside and creating short valleys parallel to the escarpment. It was in one of these, later blocked by landslides, where water accumulated to create Lake Gormire.

Although thousands of visitors view the lake from the Cleveland Way, very few attempt the walk down to it. It remains largely isolated with only the hardy few admiring its dark waters from the shore. Perhaps it is this isolation which has given rise to tales that are told. The Abbot of Rievaulx once challenged a knight riding a white mare to a race along the escarpment, only to force him over the cliff to his death in the lake. The 'abbot' was the devil in disguise. This story also neatly explains the name of the nearby cliff, White Mare Crag.

Racing on the Down

It may be difficult to imagine Sutton Bank as a popular horse racing venue, but such it was from the very early years of the 17th century when in 1612 James I provided a gold cup for a race to be run on Hambleton Down **11**. In its day second only to Newmarket, the course stretched over four miles (6.4km) from near Sneck Yate to the finishing post at Dialstone Farm. Although situated at 1,000 feet (300m) above sea level, the short, well-drained

Black Hambleton.

turf on limestone proved ideal for racing and the course became one of the most popular in the country. Such was its importance that in 1740 Parliament passed an order that horse racing could only be carried out at Hambleton, Newmarket and York. By the 1750s, however, things were in decline, possibly as a result of the remote location of the course and the difficulty in getting there. In 1755 'The Hundred Guineas', one of the main attractions of the course, was transferred to York and thereafter racing at Hambleton gradually declined. The last race was run on 27th July 1811 but although horse racing has long since ceased at Hambleton, horses still exercise on the gallops and the stables continue to provide an important training base.

A Drovers' Road

From the earliest days in history men have travelled around the country either to hunt, to seek new homes, to trade or simply to explore. Routeways gradually became established and many form the basis of our modern road system. Before much of the low land was drained and cleared of scrub or woodland the favoured routes would have been on the higher, drier land.

The Hambleton Road **12** enters the North York Moors at Scarth Nick near Osmotherley and follows the high ground of the escarpment until it leaves the park near Sutton Bank. Although used extensively during the days of droving this ancient route undoubtedly dates back to earlier times. There is every reason to believe that it was in use in prehistoric times; the Romans probably travelled along it and in the

14th century the Scots would have made use of it during their frequent raids into England.

Droving, the movement of livestock on the hoof to distant markets, reached its peak in the 18th and 19th centuries. Population was increasing rapidly and with the advent of the Industrial Revolution people were moving into towns and cities in increasing numbers. The demand for beef and lamb escalated and Scottish farmers and others in the northern counties were not slow to meet the demand. Hardy Scottish cattle and sheep were driven south to markets at Malton, York, Hull, Lincolnshire and as far south as London. Geese, pigs and turkeys were also driven to market. Higher routes were favoured because of the availability of overnight pasture and the avoidance of the turnpike roads where heavy tolls had to be paid. The long journeys and rough roads took their toll on the animals' feet, which were often shod to prevent damage, and a thriving shoeing trade developed to service this need.

The welfare of the drovers' was also essential and a string of inns was established along the roads. There were no fewer than four drovers' inns along the 15 mile (24km) length of the Hambleton Drove Road. Chequers Inn, a Grade II Listed building south of Osmotherley, closed in 1945, although it continued in operation as a tearoom for a while. Along with at least one other moorland inn it was said to have had a peat fire burning continuously for over 200 years. By far the oldest of the four inns was Limekiln House, situated where the road from Kepwick climbs the escarpment to join the Drovers' road **D**. Mounds of grassed-over rubble are all that remain today of this ancient inn mentioned in records as far back as 1577. As the name suggests, there were limestone quarries and kilns in this area for burning the stone to produce lime. The last occupants left in 1890 and the remains of the building were demolished in 1953. Dialstone Farm near Sutton Bank is said to have once been a drovers' inn, as was the Hambleton Inn on the present A170; now, sadly, closed. As drovers' overnight stops, or 'stances' as they were called, were usually about 10 miles (16km) apart it would seem unlikely that both these buildings were used by the drovers.

Ironically, it was the effects of the Industrial Revolution which had brought droving into prominence that were also to cause its demise. The development of railways throughout the country meant that animals could be transported more quickly or could be slaughtered before transportation thereby reducing costs and inconvenience. By the end of the 19th century droving was at an end.

CaCO₃ – Rock of Ages

Limestone deposited in ancient seas, either by precipitation from seawater or as shell and coral remains, is one of the most common rocks on the surface of the earth. Within the North York Moors it covers large tracts of the Tabular and Hambleton Hills as well as parts of the high moorland. Jurassic in age, it has been worked for centuries for use as a building stone or burnt in kilns to produce lime for agricultural use. Almost every farm on limestone land

once had its own small quarry for its needs. Producing a thin but fertile soil, it grows a short springy turf delightful for perambulation. The local limestone varies in colour from a dark grey to the honey-coloured stone seen in buildings around Helmsley. Breaking naturally into irregular shapes, it has been used

Dry stone walls are a feature of the Hambleton Hills. As the name suggests, no mortar is used in their construction.

for building the miles of dry stone walls throughout the Hambleton and Tabular Hills. Rain water percolates quite easily through fissures in the rock and hence limestone country is drier than the high moorlands. A feature of the limestone landscape is the many dry valleys where the water that originally created them, often during the glacial era, has long since sunk underground. Most of the small quarries are now abandoned and overgrown but the demand for limestone is unabated and is now concentrated on a few large quarries elsewhere in the county.

3 Osmotherley to Clay Bank

10 ¾ miles (17.2km)
via Scarth Nick and Carlton Bank

Ascent 2,674 feet (815 metres)
Descent 2,349 feet (716 metres)
Lowest point Huthwaite Green 418 feet (127 metres)

The walk so far has been quite easy with gradual ascents and descents and many a long stretch of almost level terrain, but now the work begins! The trail largely follows the top edge of the escarpment of the Cleveland Hills with no fewer than five stiff climbs and four steep descents. Provided the weather is kind, however, this is one of the most satisfying sections of the Cleveland Way, with a variety of scenery only lacking in sea views. Long stretches of this section have been paved with large flat flagstones which make for easy walking on the flatter areas.

From the Market Cross in the centre of Osmotherley walk up North End and at the top of the hill turn left along Rueberry Lane **A**. Tarmac soon gives way to gravel and contours around the hillside. If you wish to visit the Lady Chapel look out for a path up to the right but return to the Cleveland Way by the same route.

At Chapel Wood Farm **B**, you may wish to detour down a footpath to the left to visit Mount Grace Priory **15** which is owned by the National Trust and

operated by English Heritage. This is one of only a handful of Carthusian monasteries in England and is probably the best preserved. The detour is a mile (1.6km) return and drops 330 feet (100m). Return to the Cleveland Way by the same route.

Continue past the farm on a grassy track, go through a field gate, then a kissing gate before bearing right uphill **C**. As well as the Cleveland Way you are now following the route of the Coast to Coast Walk, a walk from St Bees on the west coast of England, which passes through three national parks to end on the east coast at Robin Hood's Bay, a location you'll be visiting in the days ahead.

The path climbs up through attractive birch woodland and passes by a number of old stone quarries before arriving at the top of the hill. Walking parallel to the wall, you now pass a television booster station on your left, largely hidden by trees, while a little further on to your right, where the wall ends, you will see the triangulation pillar or trig pillar which marks the summit of Beacon Hill at 981 feet (299m) above sea level.

From here there are good views back to Black Hambleton and north towards the Cleveland Hills and Roseberry Topping.

A paved path now begins to descend **D** (through two kissing gates) over Scarth Wood Moor, a property in the care of the National Trust. From here you may get your first glimpse of the North Sea in the far distance.

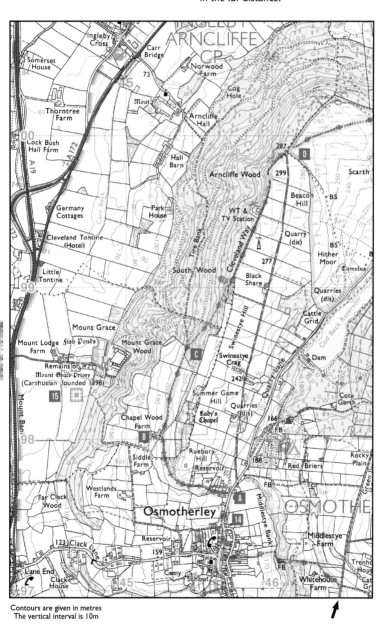

Contours are given in metres
The vertical interval is 10m

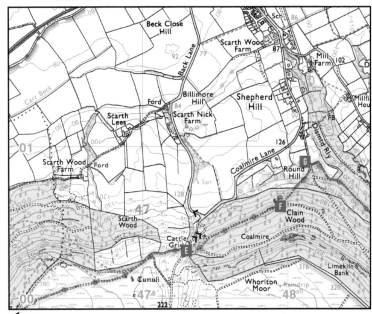

Contours are given in metres
The vertical interval is 10m

Osmotherley to Clay Bank

Follow this paved path and keep the wall on your left as you descend to the road **E**. Scarth Nick, a distinct cut in the hill to your right, was cut by water escaping from nearby Scugdale glacial lake during the glacial epoch. In more recent times the nick was also the route by which the old drove road ascended to the moors.

Turn left down the road to the cattle grid, then immediately right on a path into the woods. This route, in addition to following the Cleveland Way and the Coast to Coast Walk, is now also following the Lyke Wake Walk, a 40 mile (64km) crossing of the North York Moors from west to east.

Follow this pleasant, near-level woodland path to a point **F** where a broad path on the left leaves the forest track to descend quite steeply. Here,

on the right-hand-side, is a low carved stone commemorating Bill Cowley, who founded the Lyke Wake Walk in 1955.

At the bottom of the hill the path levels out and joins a prominent track **G** bearing left, then in a few yards turning right into the woods again.

After a fairly long level stretch the limestone rubble path ends **H** and you turn sharp left through a gate into the field. Go straight down the field to cross a footbridge and join the road where it crosses Scugdale Beck. Turn left uphill to a road junction near Huthwaite Green **I**. Go straight ahead through a gate and uphill. The path bends left along the wood edge and through another gate into the field where the bare mounds on the left are the first sign of early mining in the area.

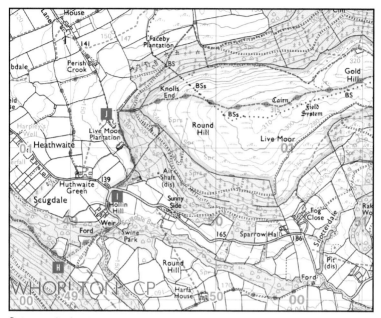

Contours are given in metres
The vertical interval is 10m

Turning sharp right **J** you now climb steeply up on a stoned path, emerging onto the moor on the flank of Round Hill. From here the path levels out a little and is paved with large slabs, making for easier going and allowing opportunity to admire the distant views. Down to the left is the prominent tree-covered Whorl Hill with the villages of Faceby to the right and Swainby to the left. The dramatic scarp of the Cleveland Hills stretches north east with Roseberry Topping still beckoning in the distance.

A standing stone on the right, carved with the letters F and W, marks the parish boundary between Faceby and Whorlton. A little further on is a large Bronze Age burial mound dating from around 2000 BC. This is a protected monument but has been damaged as a result of walkers adding stones to

the cairn. Please do not exacerbate the problem and leave the monument for others to enjoy.

The paving slabs along which you are walking were laid in the 1990s in order to reduce the severe erosion which was occuring along the route. Mainly from the old mills of West Yorkshire and Lancashire, these slabs were lifted to site by helicopter and then manhandled into place. Elsewhere in the North York Moors there are extensive stone trods of a narrower but similar nature which date back to Medieval times. These served a similar purpose to their modern counterparts in reducing erosion, but in those days were used by pack ponies, monks and other travellers on business rather than for recreational use.

From here there is a gentle climb along the edge of the hill to reach the trig pillar on the summit of Carlton Moor **K** at a height of 1338 feet (408m). Some years ago, the gently sloping expanse of Carlton Moor was the site of a glider station opened in the early 1960s. It ceased operating in the early years of this century, the buildings were removed and moorland has reclaimed the old runway.

The trail drops steeply down from the summit with wide views down Raisdale on the right. There is much evidence here for the old alum industry **16** which operated between the 18th and 19th centuries. Vast quantities of shale were removed and, after a long and complicated process, alum was produced which was in great demand in the textile and tanning industries. Jet was also mined and later carved into intricate jewellery which was very popular during the Victorian era.

Cross the road at the bottom of the hill **L** passing the Lord Stones Café & Restaurant on your right and continue ahead straight up the side of Cringle Moor. At the top there's a stone seat, another parish boundary stone and a memorial plaque to Alec Falconer, a prominent member of Middlesbrough Rambling Club, who first suggested a hill walk connecting the moors and coast as far back as the 1930s. Alec died in 1968, the year before the Cleveland Way was officially opened. His son Alan wrote the first official guide book to the route.

Carlton in Cleveland 1km or ½ mile

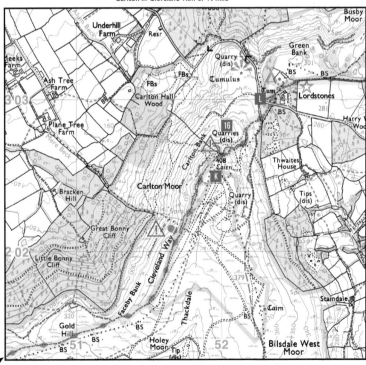

Contours are given in metres
The vertical interval is 10m

As you drop steeply down off Cringle Moor **M**, there are more extensive remains of the alum industry; you will, in fact, be walking across some of the waste tips. Towards the bottom of the hill the path bears right and then left parallel to a stone wall. Continue to ascend steeply up to the summit of Cold Moor **N**.

Heather has regenerated on Carlton Moor following the demise of the glider station that operated here until early this century.

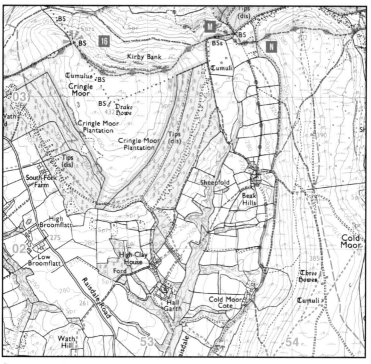

Contours are given in metres
The vertical interval is 10m

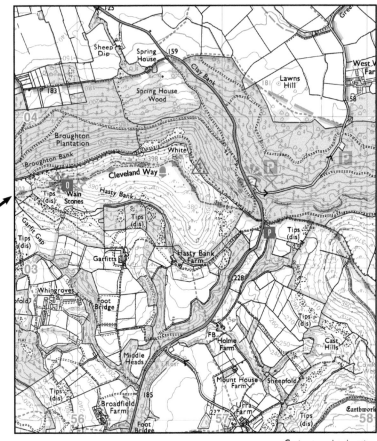

Contours are given in metres
The vertical interval is 10m

Having reached the top it's time to drop down again, this time into Garfit Gap. Where the paths diverge, take the one to the right which then swings left to climb straight uphill to the Wainstones. You may spot 'liquorice allsort' cattle on these hills. Black with a broad white bank around their middle, these hardy Belted Galloways are ideal for grazing these high, exposed hills. They also provide the beef sold at Lord Stones Café and Restaurant.

Approaching the Wainstones **O**, avoid the small path to the left and scramble

up between the large rocks. This brings you to the top of Hasty Bank and an excellent flat-paved path with glorious views down Bilsdale on your right, the Vale of the Tees and the now familiar landmark of Roseberry Topping over to the left and ahead in the distance the summit of Urra Moor, the highest point on the North York Moors.

Yet again you descend steeply through extensive mining remains, parallel to a stone wall on the right, to meet the main Bilsdale road on Clay Bank at the bottom **P**.

Osmotherley

Arriving in Osmotherley **14** along the Cleveland Way is almost like opening a door from the countryside into the town. One moment you're walking the fields, the next you've arrived in the centre of the village. Situated on the very edge of the moors and just off the busy A19, Osmotherley today is a popular base for walkers with the Cleveland Way passing through and also being close to the start of the Lyke Wake Walk. Cod Beck Reservoir, a short distance to the north, is an attractive picnic place with easy access to the moorland.

Place names ending with 'ley' usually indicate a Norse origin and indeed the name Osmotherley is thought to derive from the personal Norse name 'Asmund'. Evolving as an agricultural centre with a regular market, the opening of jet and alum works close to the village in the 17th and 18th centuries led to an increase in population. Numbers were further boosted with the opening of Cote Ghyll Mill, a weaving mill just north of the village and the Walk Mill, a bleaching mill with grounds covering some 60 acres (24 hectares) to the south. Cote Ghyll Mill closed in 1915 and after several reincarnations eventually became a youth hostel in 1980.

The centre of the village has a village cross, the base of which is Medieval, the upper part erected in 1874. A small piece of the original Medieval shaft is clamped to the wall of a nearby shop. The village also has a war memorial and a low stone table on stumpy legs called the 'barter table'. This was used as a permanent stall until the market

closed in 1823. It is said that John Wesley, a rather short man, stood on it to preach when he visited the village. Rather surprisingly for its size the village boasts no fewer than three pubs. The Queen Catherine, thought to be the only inn so called in England, takes its name from Henry VIII's first wife who gave money to enable a monk to reside in the hermitage at the Lady Chapel just outside the village.

In National Trust

Britain is blessed with probably more historic buildings than any other area of similar size, even though hundreds of properties have been lost over time. The National Trust was founded in 1895 with the aim of saving and preserving special areas of countryside, historic buildings and gardens for the benefit of the nation. The Trust is now one of the largest UK charities with huge property ownership throughout the land. On your walk along the Cleveland Way you pass close to or through a number of National Trust properties including Rievaulx Terrace and Mount Grace Priory **15** and two inland estates, Scarth Wood Moor and Roseberry Topping. Long stretches of the coast between Saltburn and Filey are now in the care of the Trust with The Old Coastguard Station Visitor Centre at Robin Hood's Bay and the Alum Works at Ravenscar being of particular interest.

The Great Ice Age

Imagine... you're standing on the top of Sutton Bank looking out over the Vale of York towards the Pennine hills. There

Mount Grace Priory lies just half a mile (800m) from the Cleveland Way. Built in the 14th century, it is the best-preserved Carthusian priory in Britain.

is ice as far as you can see. It fills the vale and reaches almost up to where you are. Now imagine you are standing on the shore in Robin Hood's Bay. You're beneath the ice sheet – the whole bay is filled with ice which reaches inland to the very edge of the higher hills.

Such would have been the scene during the Great Ice Age which commenced some two million years ago and finally ceased a mere 10,000 years before the present. The effect this ice had upon the landscape was twofold. A series

of glacial lakes were impounded in the central moorland valleys which gradually drained away to the south creating a number of impressive drainage channels. Smaller overflows to the west cut channels parallel to the western escarpment as can be seen, for example, between Sutton Bank and Hood Hill. To the east, as the ice melted, it left behind deposits of brown glacial clay which today still plasters the cliffs and gives rise to extensive coastal erosion. Such is the legacy of the Great Ice Age in the moors.

Aiming High

Walking the Cleveland Way you will pass several triangulation pillars **K** or trig pillars as they are more affectionately known. The ultimate aim of most hill walkers and climbers, trig pillars once topped over 6,500 of the high points in Britain's countryside. Today only some 5,500 remain. Most were built to the iconic Hotine design named after Brigadier Martin Hotine who was head of the Ordnance Survey's Trigonometrical and Levelling Division. In 1935 he

instigated the complete re-triangulation of Britain, replacing the old system dating back to the 18th and early 19th century. The pillar was a solid base on which to fix a theodolite used to measure angles to other visible high points and create a complete coverage of triangles over the country. Interestingly, there is nearly as much pillar below ground as there is above.

On the side of each trig pillar is an arrow or benchmark marking an accurate height above sea level. Similar arrows can be found carved into walls, buildings and standing stones, marking secondary survey points throughout the country. Now, with few exceptions, trig pillars are obsolete although they are still the responsibility of Ordnance Survey. In the 1930s survey inaccuracy across the whole of Britain was as little as 65 feet (20m) but, with modern technology, recent surveys are accurate down to within only 3mm over the same area.

Alum – A Valuable Commodity

'Take tons of shale, burn it for six months, plunge into water, add urine, boil it, dry it, use it.' This was the basic 'recipe' for the production of alum from the 17th to the 19th centuries. Used then, as it still is, in the tanning, textile, paint and papermaking industries, the production of alum in those centuries has been described as 'the first chemical industry'. Discovered in rocks in the hills behind Guisborough in the late years of the 16th century, the first quarry to exploit alum was opened at Slape Wath in 1604. Given that it could take up to 100 tons of alum shale to produce only one ton of alum and that only after many months of processing, it is hardly surprising that huge quarries gradually developed wherever the alum shale outcropped. Due to the underlying geological structure of the moors it is only north of a line from Osmotherley to Ravenscar that the old alum shale quarries can be found. The industry fluctuated over the years with some quarries closing while others opened. Remains can clearly be seen along the Cleveland Way **16** north of

Osmotherley, but the largest quarries are on the coastline where sea transport offered cheaper distribution than from inland sites. The works at Loftus and Boulby extended for over two miles (3.2km) and scoured out shale up to 200 feet (61m) in depth. Today these sites present a lunar-like landscape as vegetation has struggled to re-establish. At Ravenscar the Cleveland Way passes right through the old processing site of the southern-most alum works on the coast. Now in the care of the National Trust, there are excellent on-site boards explaining the whole process from mining to final transportation. This

quiet and attractive location on the cliff top would have presented quite a different scene when the works were in operation between 1640 and 1862. Workmen would be busy in the quarry hacking out the shale using picks and shovels before barrowing it to the flat floor of the quarry, there to be heaped into huge mounds interspersed with brushwood. Set on fire at an early stage then clamped with clay, the pile would be left to 'cook' for months before being broken open and the contents plunged into nearby water tanks. From there the liquor would be passed to boiling pans where the necessary urine would be added before the brew was allowed to crystallize in barrels. The final process was to mill the alum crystals into a 'flour' then bag it for transportation – a time consuming and labour intensive process. The alum industry in Yorkshire gradually faded in the 19th century after a cheaper means of production from coal shale was discovered. In 1871 Kettleness quarry and the once mighty Boulby works closed. The scars of this long gone industry remain but have since become a part of our industrial heritage.

Hay silage provides sheep with welcome sustenance on a cold winter's day at Clay Bank.

The Wainstones, one of many local rock-climbing locations.

4 Clay Bank to Kildale

9 miles (14.75km)
via Bloworth Crossing

Ascent 982 feet (299 metres)
Descent 1,299 feet (396 metres)
Lowest point Kildale 555 feet (169 metres)
Highest point Round Hill, Urra Moor 1,480 feet (451 metres)

You are about to ascend to the highest point within the North York Moors National Park. Some effort is required as you will be climbing from 755 feet (230m) at Clay Bank to 1,489 feet (454m) at Round Hill on Urra Moor, a climb of 734 feet (224m). Once on Urra Moor, however, you can coast gently downhill to Kildale. Most of the route is along wide moorland keepers' tracks. Just before Bloworth Crossing, you'll walk a short distance along the trackbed of the old mineral railway that connected the ironstone mines at Rosedale with the blast furnaces of Middlesbrough. If the weather is clear, this is a lovely moorland walk with extensive views over the Tees Valley, across to the Pennines and south

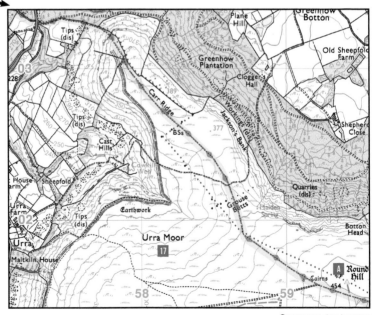

Contours are given in metres
The vertical interval is 10m

down the Vale of Mowbray. The final stretch down into Kildale is downhill along a tarmac road.

Having descended from Hasty Bank, cross the B1257 and take the signposted route opposite which climbs steadily up towards Urra Moor **17**. The path is paved most of the way to the top of the hill where a gate gives access to the high moor. There are several prominent boundary stones close to the path which soon merges into a broad track as it heads towards the trig pillar on Round Hill **A**, an ancient Bronze Age burial mound, which at 1,489 feet (454m) above sea level, is the highest point on the North York Moors.

Continue along the track which divides after about half a mile (0.8km) **B**. Follow the left hand route which continues straight ahead. Whichever way you look from this point you are surrounded by moorland and, unless there are other walkers on the route, all you will have for company are the red grouse, golden plover and a few other moorland birds.

The path gradually descends and soon turns sharp left **C**. Do not turn, instead continue straight ahead along a paved path leading up to the trackbed of the old mineral railway **18**. Opened in 1861, this railway carried ironstone from Rosedale in the centre of the moors across this high level watershed and down a mile long 1 in 5 incline, on to the processing plants on the banks of the River Tees.

Turn right **D** and continue along the trackbed to Bloworth Crossing, where the railway once crossed an ancient north–south highway. When the railway was in operation between 1861 and 1929 this was a manned gated crossing. Turning left here, **E** you leave walkers who are following the Coast to Coast route or the Lyke Wake Walk **19**.

A prominent standing stone at the side of the track **20** marks the boundary between estates, although the inscriptions are difficult to decipher. One reads 'T.A. 1768' and another 'F1838'. The name 'Sir W Fowels' is that of a local landowner who died in 1845. The smaller stone at the side is

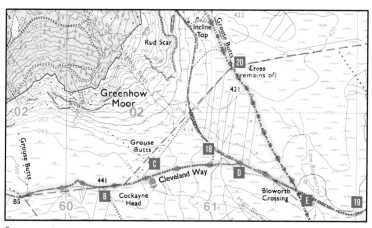

Contours are given in metres
The vertical interval is 10m

the remains of a socketed cross named 'Jenny Bradley' though nobody knows why. It is one of dozens of standing stones and crosses to be found across the North York Moors.

Another prominent burial mound, Burton Howe, is passed on the right **F**. On the relatively flat landscape of the North York Moors these tumuli are conspicuous features and are very common across the moors. A central stone slab cist containing the burial was surrounded by a circle of stones placed on edge, probably to represent the round house in which the deceased had lived. The whole was then mounded over with earth and turf.

The track rises gently up to Tidy Brown Hill **G** where you turn right through a steel gate. There are great views towards Roseberry Topping and distant Highcliff Nab, locations still to be visited. After about a mile and a half (2.4km) the track joins a tarmac road **H** which you now follow for just over two miles (3km) into Kildale. Down to the right is Baysdale **21**, arguably one of the remotest valleys

The smaller of the two standing stones is the Jenny Bradley stone. Why it commemorates Jenny Bradley remains a mystery.

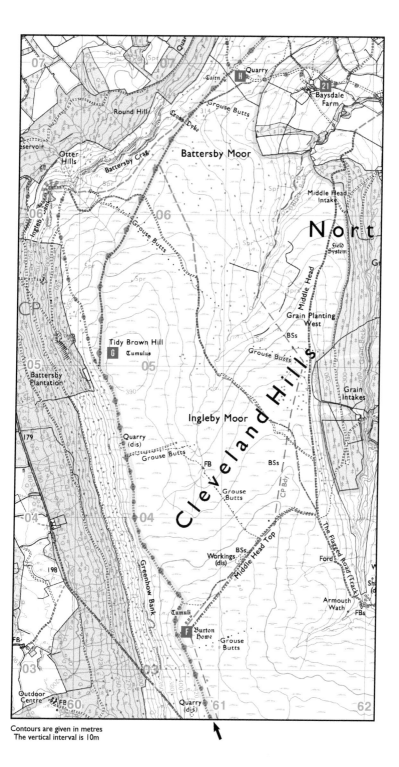

Contours are given in metres
The vertical interval is 10m

in the moors. This is where a group of Cistercian nuns decided to settle and build their nunnery in the 12th century. Nothing remains today but the name and a beautiful stone bridge over Baysdale Beck.

After an initial short rise the road crosses a cattle grid and sweeps downhill, very soon passing a dedication on a stone pillar to four young airmen who lost their lives after their plane crashed near here in 1941 **22**. Tragically, although they survived the crash, they died of exposure before they could be rescued.

Up to the right is Kildale Crag **23**, a haunt of rock climbers. The names 'The Park', 'Park Dyke' and 'Park Farm' on the Ordnance Survey map are indications that a deer park existed here in Medieval days, one of numerous such parks around the North York Moors.

The road soon arrives at a T junction on the Kildale road **I**. Turn right here towards Kildale then take the first left and continue for about 50 yards (46m) where you will find the Glebe Cottage Tearooms **24**. If they are open try a bowl of their soup, excellent whatever the weather.

Ingleby Greenhow 2km or 1 mile

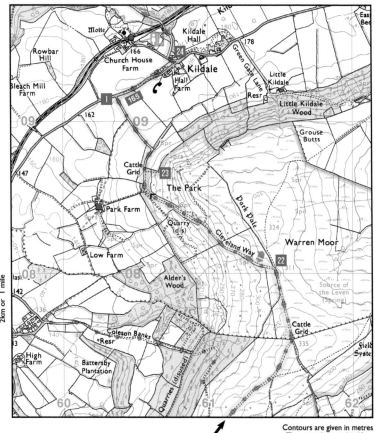

Contours are given in metres
The vertical interval is 10m

Glorious Moorland

Did you know that the heather moorlands of north east Yorkshire are man-made? Well, not entirely man-made, the shape of the landscape being determined by the underlying geology. However, were it not for man's continued influence over many centuries our glorious heather moorland would look very different. Following the end of the Ice Age some ten to twelve thousand years ago the landscape would have remained bare of vegetation for a considerable time. Gradually, however, plants began to colonise the area and eventually, by around 8,000 years ago, much of the upland was clothed in mixed woodland. From analysis of pollen found in the deep peats we know that these early woodlands consisted of pine, birch, oak and hazel. This period coincided with the arrival of the first humans to colonise the country and they immediately, although at first only gradually, began to have an effect on the natural vegetation. As the population increased over the centuries, so the destruction of the natural woodland escalated until by Roman times most of it had disappeared, giving way to heath and grassland. The changes which brought about our present heather moorland can be traced back to the mid-nineteenth century when the sport of grouse shooting became popular. The red grouse cannot be bred in captivity so careful management of its natural habitat is the only way to maintain and enhance its numbers. The bird needs young heather shoots to eat and thicker cover in which to nest and breed. The principal means to achieve this is by the controlled burning of areas of heather on a rotational plan.

It is this management which gives the moorland its checkerboard pattern. Other species which benefit from moorland management include golden plover, snipe and curlew. Hardy Swaledale sheep also graze the moors and although there are few fences they seldom roam far from their own territory or 'stray'. Introduced to the moor when they are young, they are said to be quickly 'heafed to the stray'.

The North York Moors contains the largest area of heather moorland in England and in August when the plant is in bloom it presents one of the most glorious scenes in the British countryside. This was the prime reason for designating the area a National Park in 1952. It is perhaps ironic that such a beautiful and apparently natural landscape has been brought about and is largely maintained through the hand of man.

The Coffin Walk

For about 11 miles (18km) from Scarth Nick near Osmotherley to Bloworth Crossing on the old Rosedale railway the Cleveland Way follows the same route as the Lyke Wake Walk **18**. Founded in 1955 by Bill Cowley this 40 mile (64km) walk crosses the high ridge of the North York Moors from one side to the other. The challenge is to complete the walk within a twenty four hour period, although the record crossing has been accomplished in under five hours.

At the height of its popularity in the 1970s up to 20,000 walkers a year were following the route, leading to severe erosion of some sections. After severe moorland fires in 1976 and with increasing numbers of challenge walks becoming available, numbers following the Lyke Wake Walk dropped.

Many years ago, if a church did not have burial rights a body often had to be carried a long distance to one that did. Corpse roads evolved, often over high ground, with resting places along the way. The unusual name of the Lyke Wake Walk is derived from this custom. 'Wake' meaning watching over a corpse and 'Lyke' refers to the actual corpse. It is doubtful, however, that corpses were ever carried from one side of the North York Moors to the other.

Ironstone

It may come as a surprise to some people to learn that until the 1960s ironstone had been intermittently worked within north east Yorkshire for centuries, appropriately from the Iron Age some

2,500 years ago to 1964, when the last iron mine closed. Iron Age evidence for the industry is limited but there are numerous sites of Medieval date scattered throughout the area. Ironstone was worked near to the surface from short vertical shafts which were opened into a bell shape when the iron seam was located. Brought to the surface, the stone was then smelted in small charcoal fired furnaces, the slag was run off and the iron or 'bloom' was left for working by hammering. Improvement in techniques led to the development of an early blast furnace in the 16th century which resulted in a concentration of the industry in fewer locations.

By the time of the Civil War in the mid-17th century, iron working had all but ceased in the north east and was not revived until the early years of the 19th century. The richest seams of ironstone were found in the Esk Valley and the northern hills from which vast quantities of ore were removed over the years. Blast furnaces were built, railways constructed and the new town of Middlesbrough grew up on the banks of the River Tees. In 1856 a rich seam of ironstone was discovered in Rosedale in the heart of the moors. The ore was burnt in kilns on site to reduce its weight before it was transported by rail to the banks of the Tees. The boom was not to last, however. As in the 17th century, competition, and the discovery of richer ores elsewhere led to a decline in the industry which was finally brought to a halt by the closure of the North Skelton mine in January 1964.

The Ingleby Incline allowed ironstone from the Rosedale Valley in the heart of the North York Moors to be transported out to industrial Teesside.

5 Kildale to Saltburn

14 ¾ miles (23.57km)
via Roseberry Topping and Skelton

Ascent 2,522 feet (769 metres)
Descent 3,065 feet (934 metres)
Lowest point Saltburn 0 feet (0 metres)
Highest point Captain Cook Monument, Easby Moor 1,060 feet (323 metres)

The first prominent feature on this section of the trail is the imposing monument to Captain Cook on Easby Moor, erected by Robert Campion, a Whitby banker, in 1827. The second feature is the isolated peak of Roseberry Topping. It may only be 1,050 feet (320m), but with its dramatic profile it has the ability of drawing the gaze upwards to suggest a much greater eminence. The airy walk along the escarpment above Guisborough needs care in navigation as there are a number of pathways in the forest but, in compensation, there are marvellous views over Guisborough and the valley of the Tees. The path finally drops you off the moors and out of the National Park at Charltons. From there the route heads towards the coast via Skelton, followed by a lovely walk down Skelton Beck and so into Saltburn by the Sea.

Turn right down the road by the side of the Tearooms, go under the railway bridge of the Esk Valley Railway **25** and over the River Leven, which at this point is flowing inland, away from the sea. The road continues steeply uphill past Bankside Farm. At the top of the hill turn left along a forest track **A**. In about 300 yards (275m) the track bends gently to the right **B** but the Cleveland Way continues on a path straight ahead. Winding through pleasant mixed woodland on Coate Moor, the path eventually emerges onto the plateau of Easby Moor **C** within sight of the dominant 60 feet (18m) high monument to Captain James Cook **26**. Erected in memory of the great navigator by Robert Champion, this is a prominent landmark for miles around.

Care is needed as you leave this location as there are several routes radiating from here. Look for the partly paved path leading gently downhill towards Gridale Gate car park. In a short distance you will pass a plaque in memory of another wartime tragedy. In February 1940 a Hudson aircraft crashed here shortly after taking off from the airfield at Thornaby. Three of the crew were killed and the fourth was later shot down over Germany.

On reaching Gribdale Gate car park **D** turn right for a few yards and then left to commence an uphill climb. Gribdale Gate is another nick point in the moors escarpment where glacial water flowed down into what was to become Lake Eskdale. Gribdale is also where the Cleveland Dyke cuts into the moors. The dyke is a wall of once molten lava which was forced into the surrounding hills fifty seven million years ago.

Mounds in the heather on the right near the top of the hill **27** are the remains of a Neolithic or New Stone Age long barrow, one of only a few to be found in the moors. Continue along the escarpment edge following a stone wall

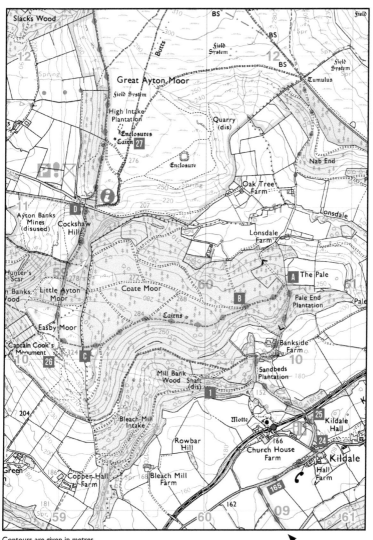

Contours are given in metres
The vertical interval is 10m

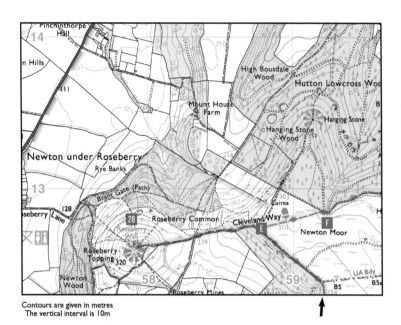

Contours are given in metres
The vertical interval is 10m

on your left as it swings around towards Roseberry Topping **28**.

You don't *have* to go up the Topping but it would be a shame to miss out on climbing 'Yorkshire's Matterhorn', and it is on the official route of the Way. Turn left through a gate **E** in the right angle of the wall and drop down to the col before climbing up the hill. At 1,050 feet (320m) the Topping may not be a mountain but the effort of the climb does not disappoint, with extensive views from the top. Looking across to industrial Teesside it is difficult to appreciate that only about two hundred years ago this was a fully farmed landscape with only a few scattered buildings. The discovery and exploitation of iron in the surrounding hills rapidly led to industrial development on a huge scale. Around the foot of the Topping the scars of this extractive industry can still be clearly seen. The farm you see down to the south, Aireyholme Farm, is where

the future Captain Cook spent many of his boyhood years before setting off for Whitby and the start of a career that would lead to fame if not fortune.

Return to the main escarpment by the same route and take the path which bisects the right angle of the stone wall by 45 degrees. Crossing Newton Moor the path joins a broad forest track **F** coming in from your left. Turn right along this track and where it joins another track at right angles **G** turn right through a gate and a motor cycle barrier. After about 100 yards (92m) turn left along a short stretch of paved way leading towards Black Nab **H**. The route ahead follows the moor edge parallel to the field boundary of Highcliffe Farm. As you follow the paving slabs, keep a sharp lookout for two pieces of broken slab about 400 yards (366m) apart carved with a date, a name, a cross and a fish **29**. See

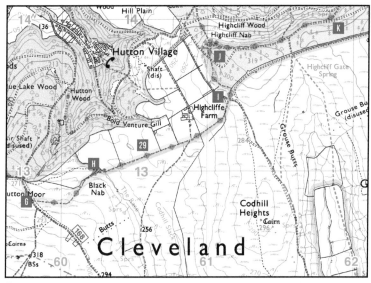

Contours are given in metres
The vertical interval is 10m

'A Mystery Stone!' on page 81 for an explanation.

Turn left through a gate at the corner of the field **I** and continue ahead though a small copse of beech trees. The path crosses a more prominent path and bears gradually up to the right below Highcliff Nab before turning sharply right to climb steeply up to the summit **J**. The views from here over Guisborough are extensive.

From here for about 3 miles (5km) the Way virtually follows the edge of the escarpment until it begins its descent towards Charltons. There are, however, numerous paths off to left and right so care is needed with navigation. After about 50 yards (46m) the path merges with a good limestone track. Continue straight ahead, avoiding any left or right turns. Where the path forks go downhill to the left **K** and then continue ahead on the level.

Guisborough Woods are a popular location for walking and mountain biking.

The track splits again **L**. Take the less prominent route on the left before gradually rising again and then turning sharp right uphill to join a more prominent track **M**, where you bear left. Within 50 yards (46m) keep left. After about a mile (1.6km) leave the main path **N** and branch left downhill before bearing right again on a less prominent path through the young forest plantation.

Join a broad grass track coming in from the right **O**, turn left downhill, then look for a path to the right leading through a handgate and into the woods. This soon joins a ribbed concrete road **P** where you turn left downhill. Where the concrete gives way to tarmac turn sharp right **Q** into the woods and follow this undulating path through the old alum quarries. This area is used for motor bike scrambling but the route of the Way is clearly marked as you descend to the old road near Charltons **R**.

Turn left along the old road, then cross the main road before turning right over the bridge, with the Fox and Hounds on your right. Bear left in front of the row of houses **S** and take the path by the side of the last house which swings up into an old quarry. Opened in 1604, this is thought to be the first alum quarry to come into operation in Yorkshire. Steep steps take you to the top of the quarry, then turn right **T** through woodland and along the field edge. At the end of the field **U** turn sharp right uphill. The route now levels out, following a broad farm track past Airy Hill Farm and down a lane into Skelton Green.

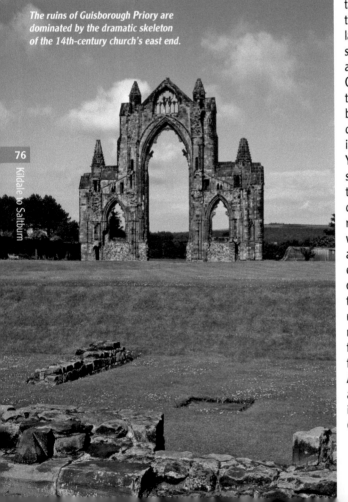

The ruins of Guisborough Priory are dominated by the dramatic skeleton of the 14th-century church's east end.

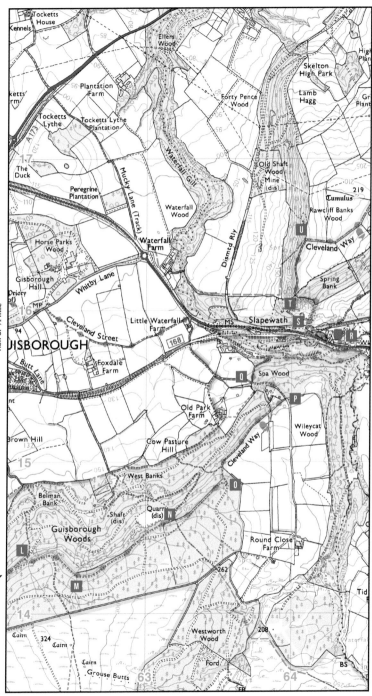

Tocketts House
Kennels
Ellers Wood
Skelton High Park
High Plan
ketts Farm
Plantation Farm
Forty Pence Wood
Lamb Hagg
Gr Plant
Tocketts Lythe
Tocketts Lythe Plantation
17
The Duck
Peregrine Plantation
Waterfall Gill
Old Shaft Wood Mine (dis)
Tumulus 219
Rawcliff Banks Wood
Waterfall Wood
Mucky Lane (Track)
U
Cleveland Way
Horse Parks Wood
Waterfall Farm
Disntd Rly
Gisborough Hall
Priory (of)
Whitby Lane
Spring Bank
16
MP
Cleveland Street
Little Waterfall Farm
MS
Slapewath
T
S
GISBOROUGH
94
Butt Lane
Foxdale Farm
168
Q
Spa Wood
P
Old Park Farm
Wileycat Wood
Brown Hill
Cow Pasture Hill
Cleveland Way
15
West Banks
O
Belman Bank
Shaft (dis)
Quarr (dis)
N
Round Close Farm
Guisborough Woods
L
262
M
14
Cairn 324
Cairn
Westworth Wood
208
Tid
Cairn
Grouse Butts
63
Ford
64
BS

1km or ½ mile

Contours are given in metres
The vertical interval is 10m

Continue ahead and cross the main road **V**. A fenced tarmac path now takes you to an open view point overlooking Skelton. A short distance beyond here some steps on the left drop you down to the main road **W** which you cross into Coniston Road.

Within a few yards turn first right into Derwent Road and follow this round and down to the bottom of a cul de sac. A gap in the fence leads you diagonally across open ground **X**, over a road and into a housing estate. Passing under the Skelton-Brotton bypass you enter woodland on a path leading down to

Skelton Beck. Cross the footbridge and pass under the impressive eleven-arched Skelton Viaduct **Y** which carries the coastal railway, transporting steel from Skinningrove Works and potash from Boulby Mine to Middlesbrough.

Soon after passing under the viaduct the path swings left uphill and then, at a decorative and welcome seat, it turns right to follow an undulating route through pleasant woodland. At the Woodland Visitor Centre **Z** strike up to the left to join the road where you turn right along the edge of the valley. Follow the road round to the right and

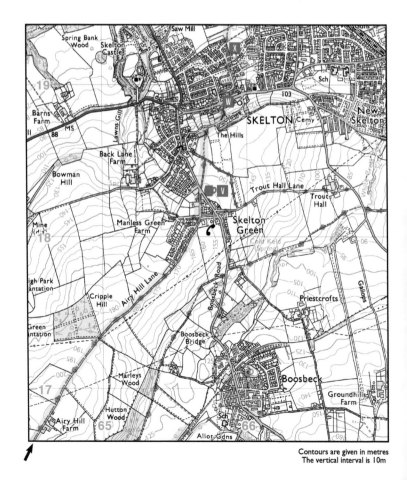

Contours are given in metres
The vertical interval is 10m

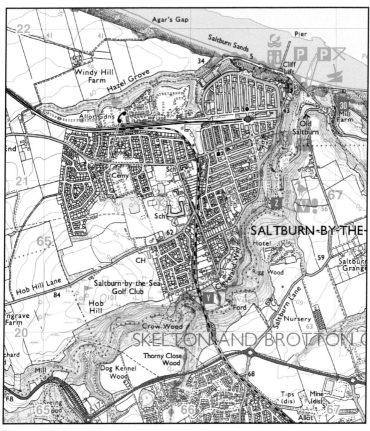

Contours are given in metres
The vertical interval is 10m

Cherry blossom in spring makes an attractive exit from the Valley Gardens for Cleveland Way walkers.

you will pass an elegant 'Victorian' bandstand constructed in 1997. This is also the location of a former bridge which once crossed the valley from east to west. 120 feet (36m) high and 650 feet (198m) across, it was built in 1868 in anticipation of building development on the east side of the ravine. This never came to fruition and after the elements had taken their toll, the bridge was demolished in 1974. Continue towards the sea and at the first building on your right a flight of steps takes you down to the seafront **30**. Alternatively simply follow the road ahead.

The Esk Valley railway line offers a superbly scenic journey across the North York Moors on its way to Whitby, and crosses the Cleveland Way at Kildale.

The Esk Valley Railway

Rural railways are almost a thing of the past but the one you pass under near Kildale is thriving. The Esk Valley Railway **25** follows the beautiful valley of the River Esk for nearly 36 miles (58km) from Whitby to Kildale then onwards to Middlesbrough. Under threat of closure on more than one occasion, it has survived and indeed has extended the number of stations on the line to eighteen, to accommodate passengers visiting the James Cook University Hospital. Although now a single line, the route was made up of several sections gradually linked up over a number of years. The oldest part is the 6 mile (3.5km) length between Whitby and Grosmont which was originally part of the Pickering Whitby railway opened in 1836. Other sections were opened in 1861 and 1865, until a final link to Middlesbrough was made to complete the line now known as the Esk Valley Railway.

Captain James Cook

While walking the Cleveland Way you will first encounter reference to James Cook soon after leaving Kildale, as you approach a monument to this great navigator on Easby Moor **26**.

Continuing on towards Roseberry Topping you can look down towards Aireyholme Farm and Great Ayton. Later, when walking along the coast, you will pass through Staithes and onwards to Whitby. All these places have strong links to Cook. Nearly 300 years after he was born in a humble cottage at Marton, now a part of Middlesbrough, his name and reputation are as strong as ever. One of the greatest navigators and surveyors the world has ever seen, Cook not only circumnavigated the world but also left behind maps and charts that have required little improvement to this day. Born in 1728, he was eight years old when the family moved to Aireyholme Farm in the shadow of Roseberry Topping. Schooled at nearby Great Ayton, by sixteen he was working in a general store in Staithes and two years later became apprenticed to a shipowner and master mariner in Whitby. The next few years were spent 'before the mast' sailing on various vessels plying the North Sea trade. After joining the Royal Navy in 1755 Cook's career spiralled as his abilities were recognised. Following survey work in North America he was selected to lead an expedition to the South Seas in 1768. This was to be the first of three voyages of exploration and discovery, all in Whitby-built ships. It is mainly on the product of these voyages that Cook's reputation stands. Tragically, he was killed on the island of Hawaii in 1779 at the age of just fifty one.

A Mystery Stone!

The Cleveland Way is a very popular walk, many people completing the whole route and others walking short sections. Wear and tear has led to severe erosion on parts of the path which have now been paved with stone from West Yorkshire. In many ways this process replicates the stone trods or pannierways which date from the mediaeval period and are a feature of many parts of the North York Moors. Both then and now, this work has contained the erosion and made for more comfortable walking for all. In the past local stone slabs would have been transported by pannier ponies; in modern times helicopters deliver the stone to site, but hard labour is still required to haul the slabs into place for a secure footing. As you walk the route between Roseberry Topping and Charltons you may notice the two pieces of broken carved stone forming part of the path **29**. The full inscription reads, 'Holy Trinity School. 15th April 1961. This stone was laid by Mrs O.G. M. Hirst. Deus Noster Refugium' (God is our refuge). Where was this school, who was Mrs Hirst and how did the stone come to rest on the Cleveland Way? Research has found that the stone came from Holy Trinity Secondary School in Halifax which moved from Savile Hall to a new site following construction in 1961. On April 17th 1961 a report and photograph appeared in the Halifax Courier headlined 'New Holy Trinity Secondary School foundation stone laid'. Mrs Hirst is described as 'a vice chairman of the Appeal Fund'. By the 21st century the school had outgrown the 1960s building and in 2010 an application to demolish it and build a new one on the same site was approved. The foundation stone became part of a consignment purchased for paving parts of the Cleveland Way. The mystery is solved!

Saltburn-by-the-Sea

Walkers on the Cleveland Way arrive in 'new' Saltburn on the cliff top. What little remains of Old Saltburn lies closer to sea level **30**. The new town owes its origins to iron and the arrival of the railway. Before 1860 this *'nasty bleak cold place'* as one gentleman described it, was farming country. The discovery and exploitation of ironstone in the nearby Cleveland Hills in the early 1800s led directly to the development of Middlesbrough and in turn to the establishment of Saltburn. Henry Pease was a member of a prominent local Quaker family which had extensive business interests including mines, railways and wooden mills. Family members played a prominent role in local politics as well as having philanthropic interests. It was Henry Pease who had the idea to establish a *'resort for the wealthy'*. Saltburn was born. The arrival of the railway in 1861 also allowed the working classes to spend a day or more in the bracing sea air of the new town.

Two of the town's most impressive features are the pier and the cliff lift. The pier, 1,500 feet (457m) long when opened in 1869, was an immediate success with thousands of visitors strolling along its length. Over the years, however, the sea took its toll

on the structure and by the 1970s it was in such a dangerous state that an application was made for its demolition. Fortunately for the town the application was refused, a renovation programme was financed and although now shortened to less than half its original length, (681 feet/206m) the pier was reopened in all its glory in 1978. The means of getting visiting Victorians from the station to the pier was greatly enhanced when in 1884 the new Saltburn Cliff Lift was opened. This inclined tramway, operated by an ingenious water balance system, is thought to be the oldest of its kind in the country and, like the pier, is still going strong.

Our Heritage Coast

Nowhere in Britain is more than seventy miles (113km) from the sea and our coastline extends for over 10,000 miles (16,000km). Our geology is more varied than any other country of similar size in the world. Little wonder then that we enjoy such a diverse coastline. Over one third of the English and Welsh coastline is now protected as Heritage Coast. The Heritage Coast concept was formulated in the 1970s with the objective of identifying and conserving the finest stretches of undeveloped coast and improving access and facilities to help people enjoy them.

Not only is most of the coast section of the Cleveland Way within the North York Moors National Park, it is also part of the North Yorkshire and Cleveland Heritage Coast. A double accolade for this magnificent stretch of England's varied coastline.

Kildale to Saltburn

Roseberry Topping.

6 Saltburn to Staithes

8 ¼ miles (13.2km)
by Skinningrove and Boulby Cliffs

Ascent 1,785 feet (544 metres)
Descent 1,770 feet (540 metres)
Lowest point Saltburn/Skinningrove 0 feet (0 metres)
Highest point Boulby Cliff 666 feet (203 metres)

From Saltburn keep the sea on your left and in just under 50 miles (80km) you'll arrive in Filey at the end of your walk. The trail is nearly always close to the cliff edge. All cliffs are dangerous, so stay on the path and take special care in windy weather. Remember, your safety is your responsibility. The Coast Path (as it was originally called) is now part of the England Coast Path, which when completed will cover the entire coastline of England. This section of the Cleveland Way commences at sea level and reaches its highest point at Rock Cliff, close to the trig pillar at 699 feet (213m). You'll see evidence of old industrial sites along the cliffs as well as locations of more recent industrial works. Modern sculptures and ancient sand dunes all add variety to the day. There are numerous ups and downs along the way, but the bracing sea air will fill your lungs.

Turn right along the seafront towards the Ship Inn, noting the old mortuary on the right. Before the invention of the steam engine, sailing ships were the main means of travel and transport by sea. Shipwrecks were a common occurrence and drowning was an accepted risk. From the car park at the back of the inn **A**, avoid the tarmac path and take the steps up to the left. A convenient Heritage Coast boundary stone **31** at the top of the steps offers a good opportunity to catch your breath and look back to admire Saltburn. The coastal path now continues along the cliff top, passing the old coastguard cottages on the right and the nature reserve of Huntcliff on the cliff slopes to the left.

After about one mile (1.6km) a plaque on the left marks the site of the Roman signal station **32** which occupied this cliff top over 1,600 years ago. Due to coastal erosion very little of the site remains. From here there are extensive views northwards towards Hartlepool, Sunderland and, on a clear day, Souter Lighthouse near the mouth of the River Tyne, over 30 miles (48km) away. Looking south west you will also see Roseberry Topping, which you no doubt climbed some time ago.

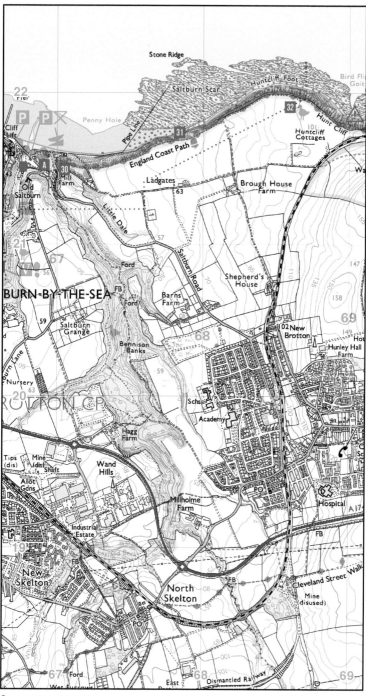

Contours are given in metres
The vertical interval is 10m

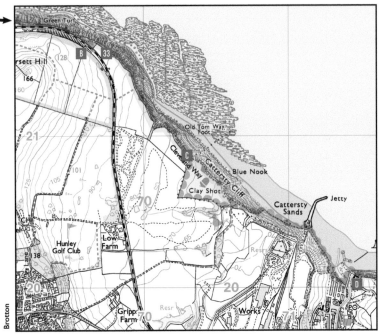

Contours are given in metres
The vertical interval is 10m

Saltburn to Staithes

The path now hugs the cliff-edge with the railway on the right hand side **B**. Potash from the nearby Boulby Mine is transported to Tees Port along this line. Look out here for three large metal sculptures erected in 1990 to celebrate the history of ironstone mining in the area **33**. From the prominent 'charm bracelet' there are good views of your route ahead towards Skinningrove and the mighty Boulby Cliffs in the distance.

As the path gradually descends, you will see the large concrete remains of a fan house once used to ventilate the nearby ironstone mines which operated from 1872 to 1906. A signpost turns you left **C** down a flight of steps towards the beach, where the path meanders through the only sand dunes on the Heritage Coast. The cliffs above you are composed largely of slag, once tipped as molten waste from the old ironworks above. Head towards the gap in the old pier, then bear right along a good track which brings you into Skinningrove. Walk along the seafront, turn left, cross

Rock cliff near Boulby, the highest point on the east coast of England.

the bridge and where the road swings up to the right **D** take the steep steps up the cliff ahead.

You'll probably want to pause at the top and this is a good excuse to look back over the village, the massive old pier and the modern steelworks on the cliff top. Once you have caught your breath, continue along the cliff path and in approximately one mile (1.6km) turn right up the field edge **E** to join a farm track. Turn left and continue between the farm buildings **F**, before bearing slightly right up to a hand gate. There's a good seat here for a rest and also an interesting panel about the work of geologist Lewis Hunton. Hunton studied ammonites in the local quarries and soon came to realise that certain species were only found in specific strata, a principle first expounded by

William Smith in the late 1700s. This enabled Hunton to accurately map the strata over a wide area. He was only 21 years old when he read a paper to the Geological Society of London in 1836, outlining his discoveries. Sadly, he died of tuberculosis just two years later. Continue through the next hand gate and follow the path which gradually climbs up through the bracken towards the top of the hill.

Approaching the hill top **G**, take care to stay on the cliff edge path, avoiding going down into the old alum quarries below. Continue along the cliff top where in about half a mile (0.8km) the path drops a little and curves around a shallow valley. While of no particular visual significance, this is where you cross the boundary to re-enter the North York Moors National Park.

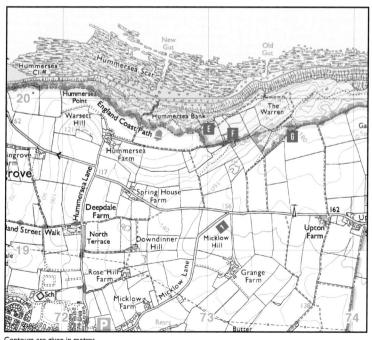

Contours are given in metres
The vertical interval is 10m

Climbing gradually uphill, the path now takes you towards the highest sea cliffs on the east coast of England at nearly 700 feet (213m) above sea level. From here there are magnificent views of the route ahead, with Staithes in the near distance. Below you are the remains of the extensive alum quarries which were in operation during the 18th and 19th centuries.

A trig pillar in a field on the right marks the highest point of land along this coastline; it's now downhill all the way to Staithes. Skirting very close to the edge of the old quarry the path bears left downhill back towards the cliff edge

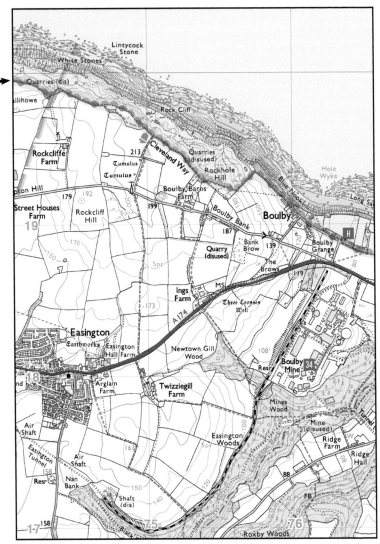

Contours are given in metres
The vertical interval is 10m

before turning sharp right towards a row of cottages at Boulby. The route goes along in front of the cottages and down the tarmac road. Where the road turns right **H** continue straight ahead down a grass path. Over to your right is the dominant Boulby potash mine **34**, opened in 1973 and still providing fertiliser for the farming industry.

The path crosses a field to rejoin the cliff edge **I**. Parts of the road between here and Cowbar have dropped into the sea on many occasions. Follow the remains of the old road to Cowbar and go steeply downhill towards Staithes **35**. Cross the footbridge and continue straight ahead along the road through the village.

The view from Boulby Cliff looks out towards Cowbar Nab.

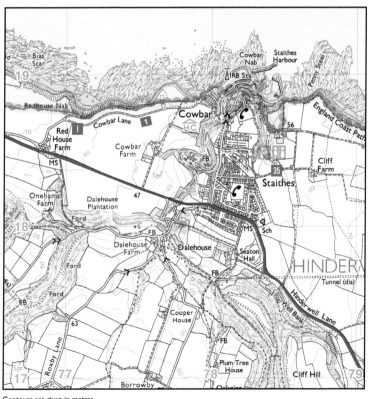

Contours are given in metres
The vertical interval is 10m

Saltburn to Staithes

A Walk for all Reasons

The Cleveland Way was opened in 1969, becoming the second National Trail in the country. Along with other coastal National Trails in England, it will form part of the England Coast Path, due to be completed in 2020. Legislation approved in 2000 allowed the creation of a route to link the existing coastal paths and also to provide for 'roll back' when erosion destroys the route. Covering 2,795 miles (4,500km) the England Coast Path will be the longest coastal path in the world. If you add the 870 miles (1,400km) of the Wales Coast Path you can walk for nearly 4,000 miles (6,436km) with the sea on your left (or right!). The England Coast Path is also the most diverse in geology and scenery. The unique geology of England displays rocks from all the major geological formations and this in turn gives rise to the varied coastal scenery from ancient towering cliffs to youthful mud flats. So, after you have completed the Cleveland Way, there are only 2,686 more miles (4,321km) to enjoy!

Romans on the Coast

Although the Romans landed in Britain in 55BC they had little affect in the north of England until some one hundred years later. Over 200 more years were to pass before they found the need to make their presence felt along the Yorkshire coast. By 360 AD sea raids by Saxons, Picts and Franks obliged the Romans to establish a chain of lookout forts along the cliffs. These were simple, defended watch towers from which signals could be passed either to the fleet or to the inland garrisons of Malton and York.

Coastal erosion over the past centuries has all but obliterated the remains of these sites. The first you pass on the Way is just south of Saltburn, although it is easily missed **32**. The site at Goldsborough near Kettleness, although complete, is only a series of mounds and bumps in a field a little way inland. Nothing is to be seen at Ravenscar, but on the castle headland at Scarborough the plan of most of the fort is still intact. The final location along the Way is at Filey where, if you walk out along the Brigg at the end of your walk, you will pass over what little remains of this once important Roman signal station.

Art on the Cliff Top

The first two of the three sculptures alongside the Cleveland Way at Huntcliff are easily missed **33**. The 7 foot (2m) diameter 'charm bracelet' is, however,

The shag – a dark, goose-sized, long-necked bird – is similar to but smaller than the cormorant.

unavoidable, even on a misty day. The work of sculptor Richard Farrington, they were erected in 1990 as part of a local arts project linking sculpture and the environment. Richard lived and worked for three months in the local community and manufactured the art works in the nearby Skinningrove steelworks. The area has a strong link with the early ironstone industry, hence the medium Richard chose to work with. The large ring of the 'charm bracelet' represents a new type of pit prop and the ten 'charms' suspended from it all have a link with the local area.

The horse charm represents the Cleveland Bay, a famous local breed, the pigeon reminds us of a traditional local pastime and starfish are common on the local shore, as is the mermaid's purse and the egg case of the dog fish. The long pointed belemnite is a common fossil found in the local Jurassic rocks. In the 14th century cats were apparently hunted in this area hence the locally named Cat Nab and Huntcliff. According to local tradition a merman (or was it a mermaid?) was once washed ashore on Skinningrove beach and the depiction of protoplasm represents the basis of life. Finally, the hammer links to local ironworking and the ring to the seafaring activity of the area.

The Saltburn to Whitby Railway

Walking south from Saltburn the Cleveland Way soon passes alongside a railway line **B**. This was once part of the line linking Saltburn and Whitby which opened in 1883. Although most of the line was closed in 1958, the section from Saltburn to Skinningrove

was retained in order to service the steel works. The following section onwards to Boulby was reinstated in 1974 to transport minerals from the newly opened potash mine.

You next encounter the remains of the line after climbing up out of Runswick Bay where an embankment runs close alongside the walk. Just beyond Kettleness the line sweeps in from your right where you cross a stile. Only a few yards further to your right is a cutting and tunnel entrance which carried the line through to a ledge cut along the cliff face. From there, having followed the ledge for some distance, the line entered a second tunnel 1,652 yards (1,510m) long, which brought it into the old Sandsend alum quarries. The Cleveland Way follows this track bed to Sandsend. The line then crossed the two becks at Sandsend on high level viaducts, the base pillars of which may sometimes still be seen in the stream beds. Following what is now the Sandsend-Whitby road, the line then cut across the golf course to enter Whitby station via a steep incline.

Potash and Dark Matter

Approaching Staithes from the north along the Cleveland Way one can hardly miss the towering chimneys and high buildings of Boulby Mine **34**. Opened in 1973 amid much controversy (it is just within the North York Moors National Park) the mine has been producing potash and rock salt in huge quantities ever since. Still the deepest mine in the UK and one of the deepest in the world, the workings reach a depth of over 4,500 feet (1,371m). High roadways and caverns extend for many miles underground and out beneath the North Sea. The valuable salts being mined were originally deposited as desert seas gradually evaporated around 240 million years ago. The demand for these salts for agricultural and road use has not abated and a new polyhalite mine is now in development on the outskirts of Whitby. Product from the Boulby Mine is transported from the site by rail, a section of the old Saltburn Whitby railway having been reinstated for the purpose. This railway parallels the Cleveland Way for a short distance south from Saltburn.

Very deep mines can provide ideal conditions for a range of scientific experiments and Boulby Mine is one of the best. Working in spaces once occupied by the potash, scientists are, among other things, trying to find out where the bulk of our universe is; apparently over 90 per cent of it is missing! Measurements taken over decades suggest that the mass of the universe is less than it appears and 'dark matter' could be the answer. To quote the Boulby Underground Laboratory website, 'Boulby is one of just a handful of facilities world-wide suitable for hosting ultra-low background science projects. Boulby is a special place for science, *'a quiet place in the universe'* where studies can be carried out almost entirely free of interference from natural background radiation'.

Staithes

Villages along the coastline of the Cleveland Way, while having many similarities, are all quite different.

'Steers' **35**, as it is affectionately known locally, lies at the mouth of a very deep gorge through which Staithes Beck flows. It is the only coastal village to have a harbour and also the only one to retain an RNLI lifeboat station. As with other coastal villages, the houses jostle for position on the limited available land, resulting in narrow alleyways between them. Staithes does in fact claim to have the narrowest street in the country, called Dog Loup. At a mere 18 inches (45cm) it is barely wide enough for a man or

Looking back over Staithes with Boulby cliff in the distance.

a dog to pass. Look out for it on your right as you turn up Church Street on your way out of the village. You'll also pass Captain Cook's Cottage, although this is not where Cook lived as a young man before he travelled to Whitby to begin his seagoing career; that cottage was washed into the sea many years ago. With luck, while passing through the village, you may see one of the local women wearing a traditional Staithes bonnet. Women once played an important part in the local fishing industry, collecting bait from the shore and preparing the fishing lines for the men. Carrying gear on the head was common practice and there is little doubt that the bonnet evolved as a practical form of protective headgear. Another form of traditional dress seen in many coastal villages is the gansey, a knitted jersey worn by the men. Close-knitted from five ply wool and without any seams, the gansey is virtually wind and waterproof. Each village developed its own distinctive pattern which could include rope, herringbone, net or waves.

7 Staithes to Sandsend

8 ¼ miles (13.2km)
past Port Mulgrave & Runswick

Ascent 1,878 feet (572.5 metres)
Descent 1,887 feet (575.5 metres)
Lowest point Runswick Bay/Sandsend 0 feet (0 metres)
Highest point High Lingrow, Runswick 328 feet (100 metres)

Staithes is the first of several attractive coastal villages that you will pass through between here and Filey. Devoted today almost exclusively to the tourist industry, these settlements present a very different face to that of a century or more ago. Isolated by the wild inland moor, their main means of communication and livelihood was the sea. Fishing and smuggling were the main sources of income with practically all the community having an involvement, including the local squire and vicar. Evidence of several old extractive industries may be seen along this coastline but nature has healed many of the scars so the signs are not always obvious.

On reaching the Cod and Lobster Inn turn sharp right up Church Street, passing Captain Cook's Cottage on your right. The narrow tarmac road ends and a path continues uphill, bearing left towards the top. Emerging at a farm, the Way turns sharp left **A** across a field to reach a viewpoint high above the village. This really is a gull's eye view of Staithes. Continue following the cliff path which soon climbs to a high

point before levelling out as it proceeds towards Port Mulgrave **36**.

Don't expect a great port here. . . its only remains today are the crumbling walls of the old harbour from which ironstone was exported from 1855 to 1917. The cliff path merges with a tarmac road and where it bends right **B** away from the coast take the cliff path on the left.

Approaching Runswick Bay **37** turn sharp right **C** by some overgrown square ponds. These once supplied water to a short-lived ironstone mine on the cliffs below and are now a haven for wildlife. Join the road by the Runswick Bay Hotel and turn left **D**. This was once the original road down into the village but after serious landslips occurred it was abandoned in 1961 and a new road was constructed, while the old one was downgraded to the present footpath.

Rejoining the road at the bottom of the hill, turn left towards the shore, then right towards the beach. Rock armour placed here in 2000 now affords easy access along the upper shore when

Contours are given in metres
Vertical interval is 10m

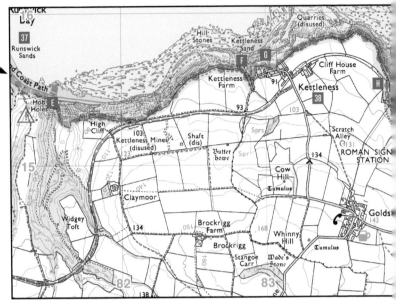

Contours are given in m
The vertical interval is

the tide is in; this is, however, only for a short distance and if you have the misfortune to arrive in Runswick Bay at full tide you may not be able to proceed beyond the rock armour. In this situation, as there is no alternative route, I suggest you enjoy a pint in the Royal until the tide recedes.

It is always pleasant to walk along a beach and it makes a change from the cliff path. Shortly after passing the wooden buildings of Runswick Sailing Club you pass a number of caves in the crumbling cliff. Do not enter! Known as Hob Holes after their resident mythical creature believed to cure children with whooping cough, these caves are actually old jet workings.

A stream now emerges onto the beach from a narrow valley **E**. Here you walk up the stream bed for a short distance, cross a footbridge and commence a

long climb up to the top of the cliffs where the path continues south as it heads towards Kettleness. A mound on the skyline marks yet another old ironstone mine and below it is the embankment of the old coastal railway.

Approaching Kettleness **38**, the path joins a farm track before passing to the left of the buildings **F** (note the five-sided wheelhouse where a horse once plodded round in a circle, providing the power to drive farm machinery). At the road veer left **G** along a grass track close to the cliff edge and after a couple of fields cross a stile to briefly follow the trackbed of the old coast railway **H**. The route eventually descends a very steep set of steps **I** into Deepgrove Wyke where it rejoins the old railway and follows the trackbed through the old alum quarries until more steps lead down into Sandsend car park **J**.

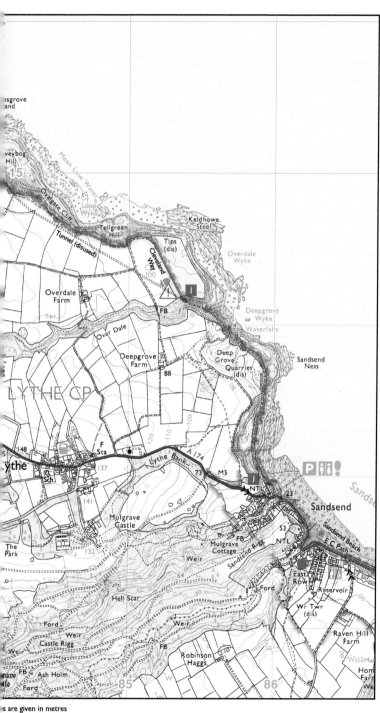

s are given in metres
tical interval is 10m

Port Mulgrave

Port Mulgrave. . . what grand visions of industry this name conjures up. A walker passing today could be forgiven for not realising there was anything special or different about this locality **36**. The more acute observer, however, may notice the scant remains of a harbour wall at the foot of the cliff or the double row of terraced cottages set back from the cliff edge, perhaps reminding him of similar rows of buildings seen in districts where mining once held sway, as was the case at Port Mulgrave between 1857 and 1930.

Ironstone quarried from the local cliffs was transported by sea from here to Jarrow on Tyneside and a harbour was quickly built to facilitate docking and loading. Sir Charles Palmer, owner of the Port Mulgrave Ironstone Company, ordered cottages to be built on the cliff top for the several hundred labourers required to operate the works. Those nearest the cliff edge were reputedly for single men while married couples were accommodated at Long Row and Short Row set further back. For their time these cottages were superior in both size and facilities to many in the area, including having their own pigsty. Set back a little on a small eminence stood the manager's house and another one, used by Sir Charles when visiting the port – a nice example of social planning.

As the ironstone reserves in the cliff dwindled, Sir Charles bought the nearby Grinkle Estate and linked his new mines to Port Mulgrave via a narrow gauge railway running in part through two tunnels. The railway and port continued in use until 1917 when the new mine was connected to the Whitby Middlesbrough railway, but by 1921 the business was in decline and finally closed in 1930.

When the harbour machinery was being removed in 1934 the wooden gantry caught fire and was destroyed. The final ignominy occurred in 1939 when the Royal Engineers blew up the outer wall of the harbour to prevent its possible use by invading German forces. Since then nature has taken its course which is why, apart from the cottages, you could pass by with no knowledge of the past history of the grandly named Port Mulgrave.

Runswick Bay

Of all the small coastal villages you pass through on the Way, Runswick Bay **37** lays claim to be the prettiest. With its many whitewashed, red-roofed cottages, colourful kayaks and surfboards pulled up on the slipway and the wide stretch of golden sand, it is difficult to disagree.

Like the other villages, however, 'prettiness' would not have been an accolade bestowed on Runswick a couple of hundred years ago. A tightly knit fishing village with every house and cottage occupied and with some twenty cobles (traditional fishing boats) in regular operation, this was a working community. 'Prettiness' has come with the decline of its traditional industry and the arrival of the new: tourism.

Today's car-borne visitors arrive in the village down a 1:4 (25 per cent) hill. Walkers will take a winding and less steep route to the shore. This in fact is the old road to the village which, due to severe land slipping, had to be closed and the present route built in 1962. Landslides are not uncommon along this coastline. A major slip in the mid 17th century took all but one house in the village into the sea. The tale is told that at the time the villagers were attending a wake when the disaster occurred. All escaped unharmed, but the only house remaining was that of the dead man!

Sea Harvest

Fishing has played a large part in the life of our coastal settlements for centuries, all the villages and towns having originated as fishing communities. Today the industry is only a shadow of its former self. However, the colourful Yorkshire coble will still be seen as you walk along the coast. The coble traces its ancestry back to the days of the Vikings. With its flat bottom, high bow and cut away stern, it was designed to be launched from the beach straight into the surf and on return would often be manoeuvred to allow the coble to be beached stern-first. The coastal herring fishing industry is long gone but crab, lobster and white fish still provide a small income for local boats.

Birds of the Sea

Many seabirds are quite large and frequently flock together, a great advantage when trying to identify them. The ubiquitous herring gull is heard as well as seen all along the coast, but beware if eating fish and chips in Whitby or Scarborough as these voracious gulls will quickly gobble your lunch! By contrast the kittiwake will only be seen in spring and summer when large colonies nest on the cliff faces and are particularly easy to see while walking round the

Runswick Bay was once important for its fishing, but only a small amount takes place today.

RUNSWICK BAY

Castle Headland in Scarborough. Their cries of 'get away, get away, get away' are quite deafening as they wheel and swoop about the cliff face. By contrast the more independent fulmar often nests alone on the higher reaches of the cliff face and may be seen at any time of the year. Related to the albatross, this bird can glide for hours over the sea with hardly a wing beat and with apparently very little effort. Beware if you get too close to a fulmar; as a defence it can eject its stomach contents with some accuracy! The black-headed gull is more often seen along the coast in winter as it spends the spring and early summer on inland moorlands where it breeds. The dark brown head is conspicuous in summer but the colour is lost in winter. Its raucous cry is a good identification feature. Large black birds flying low over the sea or perched on rocks with wings outstretched identifies the cormorant or shag. The difference is sometimes hard to distinguish unless you are very close or have good binoculars. The cormorant is black with white on the throat while the shag is slightly smaller, has a crest and is dark all over the body. As divers they can often be seen swimming low on the surface of the sea before upending into a dive, often staying underwater for a considerable time. After a prolonged period of diving they will often stand on a rock with wings outspread to dry. The end of the Cleveland Way at Filey is one of the best places along the coast to observe sea birds and waders. The cliffs on the north side of the Brigg provide ample nesting sites while the rocky seawards promontory and sandy bay are ideal for feeding waders.

The unique formation of Black Nab is a favourite with photographers on the North Yorkshire coast.

Staithes to Sandsend

Kettleness

Blink and you'll miss it. Kettleness **38** is a tiny hamlet on the coast south of Runswick Bay but what you see today is all of relatively recent age. Most of the original village gently slid into the sea as a result of a huge landslide which occurred here in 1829. If such a slide occurred today the fossil hunters would be out in force as these cliffs are among the most fossiliferous along the coast. The scarred headland is the result of alum quarrying and processing which took place here intermittently from the 1750s to final closure in 1871.

The End of the Sand

Approaching Sandsend **39** along the Cleveland Way you follow the track bed of the old coast railway which closed in 1958. The alum quarries through which the line passed operated from the early years of the 17th century until closure in 1871. Just before the old station house the Way drops to a car park which was the site of the alum processing house, the only remains of which are the two arches by which cars now enter and leave the park.

Sandsend, the village where the sand ends and the rocky cliffs begin, is divided between two parallel valleys where Sandsend Beck and East Row Beck enter the sea. The part of the village in between the valleys is situated on the main coast road between Whitby and Saltburn and is often washed by the sea as storm breakers crash over the road. This part of the village travellers cannot miss but there is another, hidden corner that offers a marked contrast to the busy seafront. Walk up the valley at the foot of Lythe Bank and a quiet, attractive scene is revealed, with scattered cottages overlooking Sandsend Beck and backed by woods of the Mulgrave Estate.

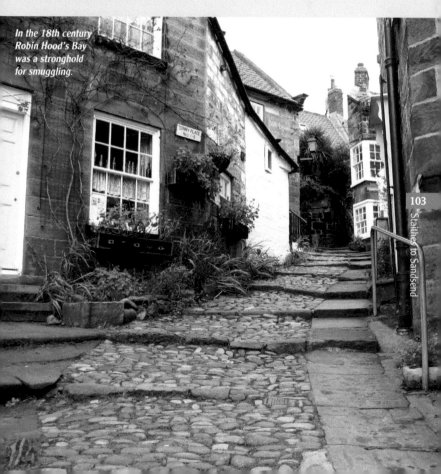

In the 18th century Robin Hood's Bay was a stronghold for smuggling.

8 Sandsend to Robin Hood's Bay

9 ½ miles (15.25km)
through Whitby

Ascent 1,607 feet (490 metres)
Descent 1,602 feet (488 metres)
Lowest point Whitby 12 feet (4 metres)
Highest point Far Jetticks 282 feet (86 metres)

From Sandsend **39** to Whitby you can either follow the road or the beach, subject to the state of the tide, but whichever route you take the distant view of Whitby Abbey will draw you on. The town itself will hold you for a while – there is so much to see here: the harbour with its bustle of vessels, the historic piers and their ancient lighthouses, the old town with its 'ghauts' and 'yards', the ancient church of St Mary with its box pews and three decker pulpit and, overseeing the whole, the majestic abbey. There are plenty of good pubs and probably more fish and chips shops here than anywhere else in the country. The walk from here to Robin Hood's Bay is one of the most popular in the National Park, particularly when followed in this direction. High cliffs, distant views and several seabird colonies add variety to a pleasant walk.

Leave the car park and follow the roadside footpath through Sandsend, crossing the footbridge over East Row Beck **A**. The official route of the Cleveland Way now follows the roadside path for just over a mile (1.6km),

passing the golf club before turning left **B** down a road opposite a caravan site and through the golf course. Pass under a high level footbridge used by golfers and veer right, climbing gradually uphill. The path takes you along the cliff top to join the road which you follow to

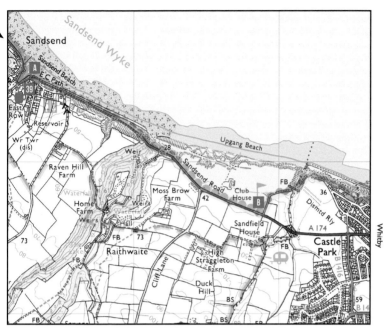

Contours are given in metres
The vertical interval is 10m

Newholm
1km or ½ mile

The coast at Sandsend is popular with families and surfers alike.

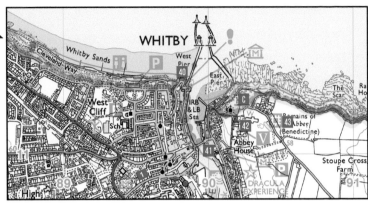

Contours are given in metres
The vertical interval is 10m

Hawsker
4km or 2½ miles

a point where a statue of Captain Cook looks out across the harbour **40**. Go through the whalebone arch and down the steps to emerge on the harbour side. Turn right and follow the road to the swing bridge.

A pleasant alternative if the tide is low is to walk along the roadside path, cross the footbridge over East Row Beck then drop onto the beach. Walk along the beach to where the rock armour begins, then join the sea wall, which can be followed to the Spa, before returning to the beach to arrive at Whitby Pier. Turn right here and walk along the harbour side to the swing bridge.

Cross the bridge and on your right is Grape Lane **41** where James Cook lived as an apprentice prior to going to sea. You turn left, however, into Sandgate which leads into Market Place, dating back to 1640 with its ancient Town Hall built in 1788. Cross the square diagonally and turn left into Church Street which leads along to the bottom of the famous 199 steps. You now have a stiff climb, counting the steps as you go. Tradition dictates that if your count

doesn't reach 199, you have to go back and start again!

At the top of the steps stands a beautifully carved stone cross erected in 1898 and dedicated to Caedmon, (c. 657–684) often regarded as the first known English poet **42**.

Walk up through the churchyard past St Mary's Church, well worth a visit if you can spare the time. Cross the car park **C** with Whitby Abbey **43** on your right to the old stone cross, then across the green to the path on the cliff edge. The walk from here to Saltwick along a good limestone path is one of the most popular in Whitby. Looking down from the cliff top you may be able to spot the remains of a shipwreck. Close examination on the shore reveals that this was a concrete ship, one of several built by the Admiralty in the First World War in order to preserve steel stocks. The Creteblock as she is known was eventually brought to Whitby in the 1930s and was abandoned in 1947. In October 1914 this was also the site of the wreck of the Rohilla **44**, a hospital ship from which 145 passengers and crew were saved after a series of heroic rescues involving no fewer than six lifeboats.

The Way continues through the middle of the Saltwick Holiday Village **D** before continuing along the cliff edge above Saltwick Bay. The unusual shape of the headlands on either side of the bay is the result of extensive excavation of shale for the alum industry in the 18th and 19th centuries. Looking down into the bay when the tide is low reveals the remains of old harbour walls.

A little further on you pass the old fog horn station, or 'Whitby Bull', whose dulcet tones once echoed out over the sea in bad weather to warn ships of the nearness of this dangerous coast. This is now a private house.

Cross the road leading to the lighthouse **E** and climb up behind it as you continue along the cliff path. As with all other lighthouses around Britain's

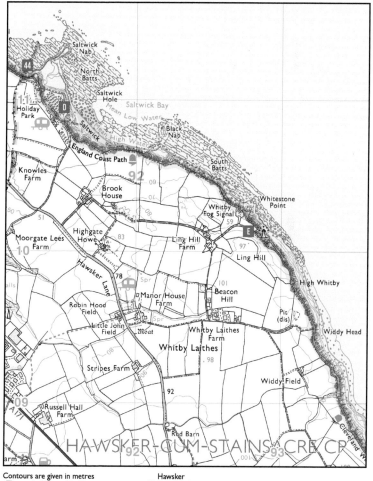

Contours are given in metres
The vertical interval is 10m

Hawsker
1km or ½ mile

The statue of Captain Cook on the West Cliff looks proudly out across Whitby to the sea.

coasts, the Whitby light is no longer manned; it was automated in 1992, six years before the last British lighthouse 'closed' in 1998.

The route from here to Robin Hood's Bay **45** clings to the cliff edge all the way so there is no chance to stray. A few steep ups and downs to cross small streams will keep the muscles in trim but the views south are a great distraction. At Maw Wyke Hole **F** the Coast to Coast walk, which you last encountered way back on Urra Moor, once again joins with the Cleveland Way to complete the last few of its 192 miles (309km).

As you round North Cheek the views of Robin Hood's Bay open up with Ravenscar, Scarborough, Filey Brigg and Flamborough Headland in the distance. Just before reaching the village there are lovely views into the village of Bay itself. In the appropriately named Rocket Post Field is a replica of a rocket post once used as a practice post for the local shore-to-ship rescue brigade. If a vessel was stranded close inshore a rocket could be fired over the ship, carrying a line. Once the line was secured on board a breaches buoy was attached by which sailors could be pulled safely ashore.

The path then passes through a hand gate and joins a road at the end of which you turn left to arrive at the car park above the old village of Bay Town.

1 km or ½ mile

Contours are given in metres
The vertical interval is 10m

Whitby Town

Whitby is a special place in so many ways. Despite being situated on the east coast it faces due north. In high summer you can stand on the cliffs and enjoy the unusual experience of watching the sun both rise and set in the sea. The town's river, the Esk, is the only one to enter the sea between the Tees and the Humber and its hinterland includes the largest area of heather moorland in England. The town's claims to fame are numerous. Whitby Abbey **43**, which dominates the town, is close to the site of an earlier abbey built in the 7th century. It was here in 664 AD that the Synod of Whitby was held which, among other things, determined when the festival of Easter was to be

The railway from Pickering to Whitby opened in 1836. Following closure in 1965 it was reopened as the North Yorkshire Moors Railway between Pickering and Grosmont in 1971, and now carries more passengers than any other steam railway in the UK. Linking to the BR line at Grosmont now allows steam trains to continue to Whitby.

held, a ruling which we follow to this day. It was in this same period that Caedmon, regarded as the first English poet, wrote his famous song which is commemorated on an ornate stone cross which you pass at the top of the 199 steps leading up to Whitby Parish Church. A new monastic settlement was established around 1078, although the ruins we see today date from the early 13th century. Suppressed by Henry VIII in 1539 and robbed of much of its stone over succeeding years, what remains today is still a very imposing structure.

The statue of Captain Cook **40** on the opposite side of the river reminds us of this great navigator's connection with the town. It was here that he was apprenticed for some years and where all four of the ships he sailed in to explore the world were built. Two other famous sea captains who sailed from Whitby were William Scoresby and his son, also called William. Scoresby senior is credited with the invention of the crow's nest which protected sailors on lookout at the mast head.

The town has a number of literary associations. Bram Stoker opened 'Dracula' with a shipwreck off the coast of Whitby, inspired by the remains of the MV Creteblock. The count escapes and, turning into a black dog, bounds up the steps towards the old church to hide in a grave. Charles Dodgson (alias Lewis Carroll) was supposedly inspired to write 'The Walrus and the Carpenter' after visiting Sandsend beach.

Shipbuilding, whaling and jet working have all played a part in the fascinating history of this old town, but the arrival of the railway in 1836 encouraged a new business, tourism, which has boomed while other industries have declined. Events take place throughout the year, from Goth Weekend and Whitby Folk Festival to Regatta Weekend, Sixties Weekend and several other crowd pullers. Even in mid winter the town may be crowded with visitors enjoying the bracing sea air and fish and chips.

Jet Black

'The fumes of it, burnt, keep serpents at a distance and dispel hysterical affections: they detect a tendency also to epilepsy and act as a test of virginity. A decoction of this stone in wine is curative of toothache; and in combination with wax it is good for scrofula' - Pliny the Elder

Jet black in colour, light in weight, conchoidal in fracture and shiny when polished, jet is the preserved remains of the monkey puzzle tree (*Araucaria*) which once grew in the ancient landscape of Jurassic times some 190 million years ago. Although found in several parts of the world throughout historic times, the best quality jet can still be collected in the North York Moors. Jet beads found in Bronze Age burial mounds on the high moors tell us that the material has been valued for its decorative properties for thousands of years, but it was not until the Victorian era that a jet industry evolved, based in Whitby.

Originally collected along the shoreline where it was washed up by the tide, jet was later extensively mined throughout the northern moors and coast using simple hand tools and very crude mining techniques. The alum industry left a huge visual impact on the landscape whereas evidence for the jet industry has to be searched for more diligently. However, as the strata containing jet is to be found immediately below that containing alum, this gives a good clue to locating the old jet mines. To mine the jet, adits were driven into the hillsides or coastal cliffs, the jet was removed and the process then repeated further along the outcrop. Waste was simply tipped down the slope below the adit or into the sea. As you walk along the escarpment north of Osmotherley you cannot fail to see the great scars of the old alum industry, below which you may notice the smaller waste tips from the jet mines.

Although popular as jewellery in early Victorian times it was the death of Prince Albert, Consort to Queen

Victoria, in 1861 that brought about a surge in popularity of jet. Victoria was to wear heavy jet jewellery for the rest of her long life.

This popularity led to a boom in the industry which in its heyday saw no fewer than 200 jet workshops in Whitby, employing over 1,500 men, women and children. The jet workers tools were simple lathes, drills, knives, files and polishing wheels. With these a skilled worker was able to produce the most intricate of designs. By the late 1800s jet was going out of fashion and this, coupled with imitations and cheap imports, led to the gradual collapse of the industry by the mid 1900s. A revival of interest in recent years supported by innovative new designs has led to jet once again being carved and sold in the town. Look in the shops as you walk along Church Street towards the abbey to see both new and old jet jewellery or, if you have time, visit the town's Pannett Park Museum which houses a wonderful collection of jewellery as well as a magnificent model of Whitby Abbey carved in jet.

Walk along the shore after a high tide and you may be lucky enough to find some small pieces of Whitby jet, but beware, there is a lot of sea coal around as well. Chemically the two are very similar, so how should you tell the difference? You could try one of Pliny's tests, but a much safer identification is to look for the conchoidal fracture lines (like broken bottle glass) or rub a piece on dry sandstone – if the streak is black you have sea coal, if it's brown you're in luck.

Whitby jet has been popular for over 150 years and the town still has a number of shops selling jet jewellery.

The Wreck of the Rohilla

The rescue of 145 people from the wreck of the hospital ship Rohilla is one of the most heroic in the history of the Royal National Lifeboat Institute. The 7,500-ton Rohilla with 229 people on board left Queensferry en route for Dunkirk on October 29th 1914. Early the following morning she ran onto rocks close inshore, east of Whitby pier **44**.

At the time Whitby could boast three lifeboats, all rowing vessels. Due to appalling weather and sea conditions, however, the No. 1 boat could not be launched. The No. 2 boat was manhandled over an 8ft-high wall and hauled along the beach below Whitby Abbey. Launched from the beach in the early morning she was able to rescue a number of people before returning for a second attempt. In all, 35 passengers were rescued but the boat was by then too damaged to continue. Whitby's third rowing lifeboat, stationed a mile west of the town, was then hauled overland and lowered down the cliff face onto the beach, but the sea was too rough to launch.

Lifeboats from Scarborough and Teesmouth were launched but were unable to assist until finally the 'Henry Vernon', one of the new motorised lifeboats, sailed down from Tynemouth, collected barrels of oil in Whitby which was poured onto the sea in the vicinity of the Rohilla and in the ensuing calm the last fifty survivors were taken on board and transferred to Whitby. Rowing lifeboats were gradually phased out in favour of motorised vessels but appropriately the last rowing lifeboat to be used on active service was here at Whitby.

The High Light of Whitby

Not many organisations survive the test of time over hundreds of years. The Corporation of Trinity House, founded by Royal Charter granted by King Henry VIII in 1514, is still in charge

of lighthouses and lightships around the coast of Britain. Standing 240 feet (73m) above sea level and just two miles (3km) south east of Whitby, the High Light **E** was constructed in 1858 to a design by James Walker. The red and white light flashes every ten seconds and can be seen up to 18 miles out at sea. The light ran on paraffin until 1976 when the system was electrified. Fully manned around the clock until fully automated in 1992, it is now remotely controlled from Trinity House Control Centre in Harwich. The Keeper's accommodation has been converted to two holiday accommodation units.

Whitby's East and West Piers each boast an early lighthouse and both are now Grade II listed buildings. The West Pier light was completed in 1831 while that on the East Pier followed in 1854. After extensive renovation, the West Pier lighthouse was reopened to the public in 2016 and you can once again climb the 72 foot (22m) tower for a birds' eye view of the harbour.

Robin Hood's Bay

Many people come to Robin Hood's Bay **45** for the first time because they are intrigued by the name, and the first question they usually ask is 'How did the village get its name?' The answer, unfortunately, is not absolutely clear. What we do know is that it can be traced back to at least 1322 – did Robin Hood ever visit the bay? The answer to that depends on whether or not you believe in Robin Hood!

Notwithstanding the mystery of the name, we know that the settlement has been in existence for a very long time. In 1535 the village is recorded as having twenty fishing boats based here, more in fact than in Whitby. Fishing was for many centuries the mainstay of the village although, with the advent of larger steam driven vessels, the trade gradually moved to Whitby. In the 1930s fishing in the respective seasons for cod, lobster and salmon constituted the 'Three Fevers' discussed by local author Leo Walmsley in his book of the same name and made into a film, *The Turn of the Tide*, in 1935.

Another buttress of the local economy for many years was smuggling. With heavy taxes on a wide range of goods from brandy and salt to silk and tobacco there was a great incentive to smuggle goods in from abroad. Although sometimes romanticized, smuggling was a dangerous and often violent activity.

Today the village relies on tourism with most of the houses in the old village being second homes or holiday cottages. A small volunteer-run museum has displays on many aspects of the village history while the National Trust Centre in The Dock concentrates on the marine and other wildlife of the bay.

Rocks & Fossils

People flock to Robin Hood's Bay for many reasons, not least of which is to study the unique geology and search for fossils. Formed from 200-million-year-old shales and limestones, the bay and its fossils have attracted geologists, professional and amateur, for decades. Laid down as soft sediments in ancient seas which covered the area all those years ago and since compressed, cemented and lifted above the waves, the rocks are now subject to the ever present action of wave and weather.

What took millions of years to create is now being slowly eroded away and the debris is being carried out to sea to start the process all over again.

Seen from the cliff top when the tide is low the rocks of the bay present a huge semi circle, curving round from North Cheek to Peak Steel. The individual beds create reefs or scars, the harder limestone forming the higher edges. This structure suggests that there was once a huge shallow dome here that has all but eroded away leaving the features we see today. To the south, cutting the dominant headland at Peak Steel, is evidence of a massive geological fault or dislocation of the strata, the formation of which has been the subject of discussion and debate for many years. Also near Peak Steel is a Global Stratotype Section and Point, or 'Golden Spike'. This is an internationally agreed reference point for the boundary of specific strata worldwide and is one of only a small handful in Britain. It's not very impressive to look at, but for geologists it is important.

Children and adults alike love to search for fossils among the shingle and loose boulders. Flat coiled ammonites, bullet-like belemnites, sea shells of all descriptions and the ubiquitous gryphaea or 'Devil's toenail' may all be found by the diligent searcher. Also in the limestones are numerous 'trace' fossils, the traces left behind by burrowing worms, bivalves or molluscs. These remains help us to paint a picture of what Robin Hood Bay and its marine life was like millions of years ago.

Whitby Abbey, St Mary's Church and the famous 199 steps from the West Cliff.

9 Robin Hood's Bay to Scarborough

12 miles (19.25 metres)
via Ravenscar

Ascent 1811 feet (552 metres)
Descent 1,814 feet (553 metres)
Lowest point Scalby 23 feet (7 metres)
Highest point Ravenscar 634 feet (193 metres)

You may be reluctant to leave Robin Hood's Bay, but leave you must. If the tide is favourable a walk along the shore makes a nice change from the cliff path. A steady climb to Ravenscar passes right through an ancient alum processing site where excellent plaques describe the works. From Ravenscar at 600 feet (183m) it's downhill almost all of the way. This is a coast of Nabs and Wykes with several descents almost to sea level. There are fine distant views to Scarborough, Filey and the chalk cliffs of Flamborough Head. After crossing the footbridge at Scalby Mills you have the dubious pleasure of walking on concrete for a mile or two as you head around the Castle Hill. Alternatively, you could sneak a ride on the open top bus and still enjoy the views.

Walk down the steep hill through the old village. This is New Road – the old road collapsed in 1780, taking a number of houses with it. The official route of the Cleveland Way south from Robin Hood's Bay follows the cliff top path. If you leave the village on a full or rising tide, you must take the cliff path route out of the village.

However, if the tide is low a walk along the pebble and sandy beach is a pleasant alternative from the cliff path and also saves several climbs. From the slipway walk along the beach, cross the first stream at Mill Beck and continue along the shore to the next valley (Stoupe Beck) where you pick up the official route once again as you climb a steep track from the beach.

About a hundred yards (91m) before reaching the slipway turn right up Albion Road (between Dollies sweet shop and the Smugglers) then turn left up Flagstaff Steps just past the fish and chip shop. Note the carved stone and the plaque on the wall referring to the old highway that once followed this route. The steps lead to a wooden boardwalk climbing onto the cliff top and a flagged path at the top. At the end of the flagged path bear right then left through a gate and along a limestone path parallel to the cliff edge.

Steps lead you down to Mill Beck, past the old water mill which ceased working in 1928. It is now a busy youth

A visit to Scarborough Castle affords prominent views across both South and North Bays.

hostel and also has a very popular café open to all. This inlet is known as Boggle Hole. A 'boggle' was thought to be a mischievous imp who lived here and in other coves and caves along the coast. Cross the footbridge, turn right at the road, then quickly left to climb up the opposite bank. The next valley you descend is Stoupe Beck, followed by yet another footbridge and a climb out from sea level.

Follow the track up to the tarmac road and after a dip and a sharp double bend look out for a stone step stile on the left **A**. This takes you onto the cliff path and past a Second World War 'pillbox'. Not many years ago the path went around the seaward side of this structure, which demonstrates the vulnerability of the cliffs in this area. Other wartime structures have completely disappeared into the sea.

Approaching Ravenscar, the cliff edge path swings inland for a short distance before turning sharp left into a small valley **B**, and crossing a footbridge where there are some huge horsetails, plants whose ancestry goes back to the Jurassic era.

You now emerge at the site of the old alum works **46** where there are a number of boards explaining the method of working and processing the alum. Take a while to wander around this fascinating old industrial site before leaving by the path at the south east corner. On the right you pass the house once used by the manager of the alum works and then join a broad track. Turn left and within a few yards bear right **C** up a narrower path which climbs steadily.

Low tide reveals the classic circular 'scars' of Robin Hood's Bay.

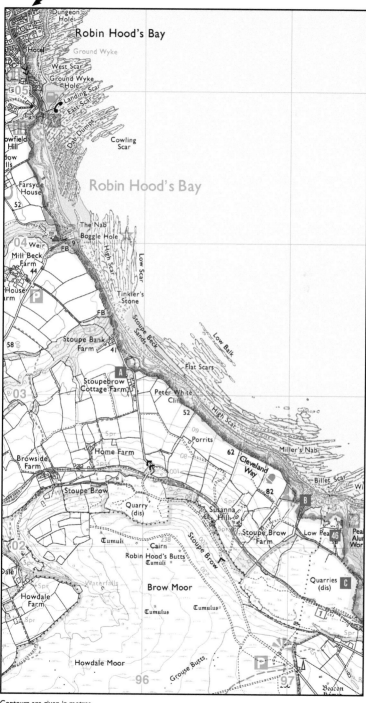

Robin Hood's Bay

Robin Hood's Bay

Contours are given in metres
The vertical interval is 10m

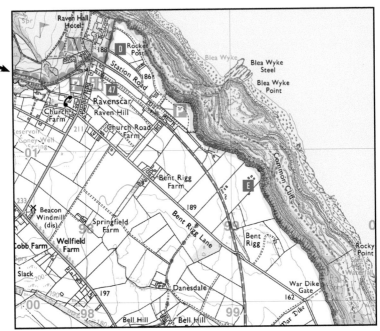

Contours are given in metres
The vertical interval is 10m

This path soon levels out as it heads towards Ravenscar **47**. Just before reaching 'The town than never was' (you've now climbed c.600ft/185m from sea level) the path is partly paved with red bricks, many imprinted with the name 'Ravenscar'. These recall the brick works which operated in the old alum quarry between 1900 and the early 1930s, supplying bricks for the proposed development of Ravenscar and, when that failed, for many buildings in Scarborough. The overgrown tunnel on the right took the railway under the Ravenscar approach road. A cutting here may have been adequate, but the landowner insisted on a tunnel so the trains would be out of sight of his house. Emerging onto the road at Ravenscar you may be lucky to find the National Trust Centre open, where a welcome cup of tea may be bought. There are also toilets just a short distance up the road to the right.

Go ahead along Station Road for about 150 yards (137m) before turning left **D** on a rough track towards the cliff edge. The old kerb stones and occasional metal drain cover are some of the remains of 'The town that never was'. At the cliff edge stop to admire the view and look down onto the shore where a large number of seals may be seen on the rocky promontory. Now turn right to follow the cliff path, passing another rocket brigade practice post. Soon after you will see Station Square over to your right where there is another convenient cafe. The route now continues steadily south along the cliff edge, passing an old coastguard lookout post **E** and the remains of a

Contours are given in metres
The vertical interval is 10m

Second World War radar station. There are good views south from Petard Point; on a clear day Scarborough, Filey Brigg and Flamborough Head may all be seen.

Steps **F** descend steeply almost to sea level into Hayburn Wyke **48**. Cross the footbridge over the beck and deviate a few yards to view an attractive waterfall cascading onto the shore.

The name 'wyke' comes from the Scandinavian for a narrow inlet. There are several along this coast. Returning from the shore pass the footbridge and continue uphill for a few yards before turning left off the main path to follow the Cleveland Way steeply up through fine old woodland. A small viewpoint part way up gives a lovely view back down to the beach. Where the path emerges onto a small, flat area take

care to bear left and continue uphill to reach the cliff edge path once again. The other path would take you a short distance to the Hayburn Wyke Hotel where refreshments may be obtained.

Continue steadily south before another steep descent takes you down to the Salt Pans. Follow the cliff path as it climbs again before descending yet again, this time into Cloughton Wyke **G**. Just before

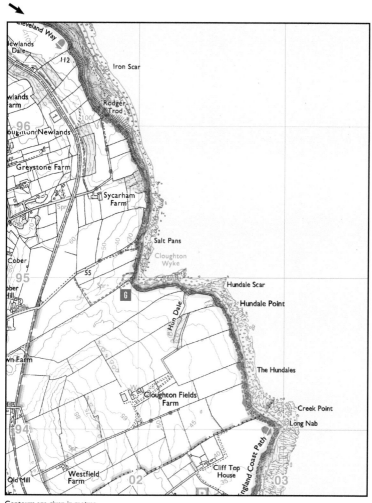

Contours are given in metres
The vertical interval is 10m

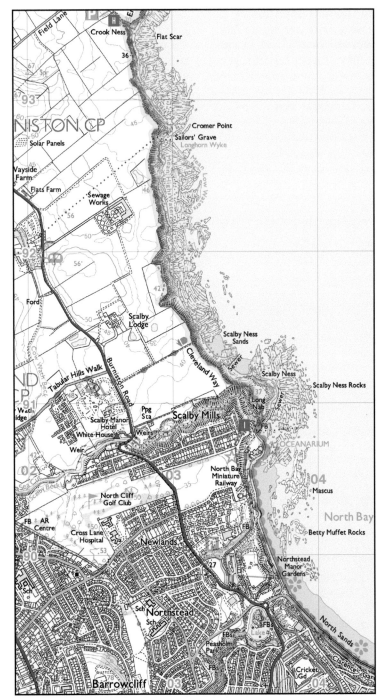

Crook Ness
Flat Scar
36

NISTON CP
Solar Panels
Cromer Point
Sailors' Grave
Longhorn Wyke

Wayside Farm
Flats Farm
Sewage Works

93
67

92

91

ND CP

Ford
Scalby Lodge

56
56
50
42
46

Scalby Ness Sands

Cleveland Way

Scalby Ness
Scalby Ness Rocks

Tabular Hills Walk
Burniston Road
Watl idge
Ppg Sta
Scalby Mills
Long Nab
FB

Scalby Manor Hotel
White House
Weirs
OCEANARIUM

Weir

02
03
04

North Bay Miniature Railway
North Cliff Golf Club
CH
Mascus

FB
AR Centre
Cross Lane Hospital
Newlands
FB
Betty Muffet Rocks

North Bay

53
27
Northstead Manor Gardens

90
Sch
Sch
Northstead
Sch
FBs
Peasholm Park
FBs
Lake
Cricket Gd
Clarence Gar

Barrowcliff
03
04
North Sands

Contours are given in metres
The vertical interval is 10m

Long Nab you cross the boundary of the National Park and approach an old coastguard lookout now used by a local ornithology group as an observation platform. Approaching Burniston Bay the path swings inland for a short distance **H** before dropping down steps to the left onto a concrete path which gives access to the shore at Crook Ness, one of the best places along the coast for finding dinosaur footprints. The Cleveland Way, however, climbs the few steps opposite to return to the cliff edge path. From here just keep the sea on your left and with only a few minor ups and downs the path soon takes you across a footbridge **I** over Scalby Beck to arrive at Scalby Mills and the Sea Life Centre. Follow the promenade to where it meets the road and the end of your day's journey.

Man the Lifeboat!

The history of Britain is inevitably bound up with the sea which surrounds it, and nowhere is this more apparent than in the story of wrecks and rescues around its coast. In the days of sail the number of vessels ploughing the North Sea would have been infinitely greater than in modern times. The sea was the highway of the time but regard for safety was often far below modern standards. Over the centuries hundreds of ships have run into problems and many mariners lost, as witnessed in the graveyards of coastal churches.

Henry Greathead is credited with building the first purpose-built lifeboat at South Shields. Appropriately named *Original,* it was launched in 1789. Others were launched at Scarborough in 1801 and Whitby in 1802. Also in 1802 the *Zetland* was launched at Redcar, and still survives as the oldest lifeboat in the world. These early lifeboats were ten-oared open rowing boats a mere 30 feet (10m) in length.

In Robin Hood's Bay a coastguard boat had been adapted as a lifeboat in 1830 and was replaced in 1839 by a specifically designed lifeboat. However, this boat had been neglected to such an extent that it was declared unfit for use when a brig, the *Visiter,* was wrecked in the bay in 1881. This event led to one of the most famous rescues in lifeboat history and also to the establishment that same year of the first Royal National Lifeboat Institution boat in the village. The RNLI had been founded in 1824.

To aid the crew of the *Visiter* a call was made to the Whitby lifeboat station for assistance, but when it was realised that sea conditions at Whitby harbour mouth would prevent the boat from getting out to sea, it was decided to haul it overland to Bay. In atrocious winter conditions the boat was hauled by horses and men through deep snowdrifts the six miles to Robin Hood's Bay. Manoeuvred carefully down Bay Bank, the boat was launched into the surf, only to be driven back after six of the oars were smashed by a huge wave. Undaunted, new oars were found and a second attempt was made, this time with success, and the crew of the *Visiter* were safely brought ashore. A happy ending to one of the most dramatic

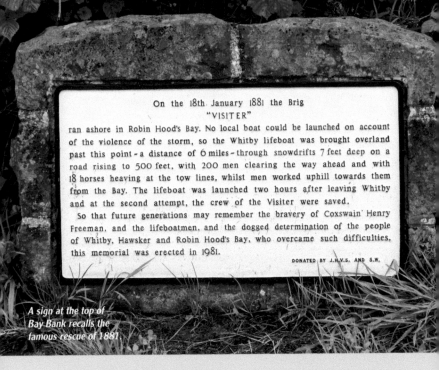

On the 18th January 1881 the Brig
"VISITER"
ran ashore in Robin Hood's Bay. No local boat could be launched on account of the violence of the storm, so the Whitby lifeboat was brought overland past this point - a distance of 6 miles - through snowdrifts 7 feet deep on a road rising to 500 feet, with 200 men clearing the way ahead and with 18 horses heaving at the tow lines, whilst men worked uphill towards them from the Bay. The lifeboat was launched two hours after leaving Whitby and at the second attempt, the crew of the Visiter were saved.
So that future generations may remember the bravery of Coxswain Henry Freeman, and the lifeboatmen, and the dogged determination of the people of Whitby, Hawsker and Robin Hood's Bay, who overcame such difficulties, this memorial was erected in 1981.

DONATED BY J.H.V.S. AND S.W.

A sign at the top of Bay Bank recalls the famous rescue of 1881.

sea rescues in the history of the Royal National Lifeboat Institution.

A metal plaque at the top of the steep road down into the old village records this historic event. And before you ask, yes, the spelling *Visiter* is correct. Although the name had long been spelt *Visitor,* local research into original records has now established the correct spelling.

'Watch the wall...'

Two centuries ago goods were secretly brought ashore from vessels plying between the continent and the east coast of England; and nowhere was this 'trade' more common than along the remote cliffs and secluded bays of the Yorkshire coast. Whichever imported goods were subject to heavy taxation

became the target for smugglers. When tea brought in from Holland costing seven old pence per pound could be sold at a sixty fold increase, when tobacco could fetch twelve times its original value and gin at least four times its original cost, it is hardly surprising that smuggling was big business. The range of smuggled goods was remarkable. As well as the more obvious items such as gin, brandy, tea and tobacco; playing cards, silk dresses, glassware and perfumed water were also smuggled into the country. Whole communities were involved in this illegal activity. Robin Hood's Bay with its isolated coast backed by wild moorland was an ideal haunt for smugglers. It is said that a bolt of silk or an anker of brandy could pass from the shore to the top

Robin Hood's Bay to Scarborough

of the village without seeing the light of day, so closely interconnected were the cottages with secret doors and cupboards. Goods brought ashore could be spirited away to remote farms for storage before onward transmission to inland towns. Smuggling was a dangerous game. Clashes between the smugglers and the Revenue officers were common and often violent – there was a lot at stake. Penalties could be hard for those captured and included imprisonment, deportation or being forced into the navy. By the late 19th century many taxes had been cut or reduced, rendering the smuggling trade less profitable and this, together with an improved coastguard service, led to its decline. If on a dark night you see a lonely light on a remote shore it is probably a local fisherman working the evening tide, or could it be a signal to some offshore vessel..? *'Watch the wall, my darling, while the Gentlemen go by!'* (Kipling)

Rocks from Afar

A walk on any of the gravel beaches along the Heritage Coast will provide an exciting opportunity to find a wide range of colourful pebbles and boulders along the upper shore. The majority of these have been washed by the sea from the brown clay which caps the harder rocks along the coastline. Much younger than the rocks on which it sits, this glacial clay was left behind as the ice melted towards the end of the great ice age some 10 to 20,000 years ago. But how did it get here in the first place?

Some two million years ago, as the climate cooled, the mountainous regions of Britain and Scandinavia gradually developed their own ice caps. As the ice slowly spread from these regions it picked up pebbles and boulders along the way as it moved to cover most of Britain, except the far south. Softer material was ground up to a clay while pebbles and boulders were rounded and polished. Moving over the flatter land this mixture was then plastered over the local topography. As the clay now erodes the pebbles and boulders are washed out to form the wonderful pebble beaches along the coast. Many of these erratics can be traced to their original source; shap granite from the Lake District, lava from Scotland, coral limestone from Northumberland, brockram from the Vale of Eden and even porphyry from Scandinavia. These all help to show us the directions in which the ice moved in bringing them here.

A Flawed Idea

Imagine living on the top of a 600ft-high (183m) cliff on the exposed coast of north east England – great on a lovely day but not so good when an easterly gale is howling in from the sea or a thick sea mist has crept up the cliff face to envelope everything in a dark, dank swirl of cloud. And what about in winter? Heavy snow could mean you are cut off from all other civilisation for days or even weeks. Hardly the ideal location to build a town, yet that is exactly what the Victorians proposed to do in 1895. Following the arrival of the railway in 1885 and its potential for increasing the number of visitors, a development company purchased the Peak Hall Estate and work began on the layout of a town that would have spread over many acres and included hundreds of houses as well as shops, golf links and gardens. A new name was created for the settlement, Ravenscar **47**, the scar of the raven, although there is no evidence that ravens were ever resident in the area. Kerbs and sewers were installed, house plots were sold and a few villas built, but in spite of all incentives business was slow and the company went into liquidation in the early 1900s.

Raven Hall Hotel, built as a private house in 1774 when it was called Peak Hall, is thought to stand on the site of a Roman signal station. Rumour suggests that King George III was brought here for treatment during his recurrent periods of madness. It is certainly known that the hall was once owned by a Dr Willis, one of the doctors who treated the King during his illness. Visit Ravenscar on a beautiful day and the views across to Robin Hood's Bay are fantastic; arrive on a cold, misty day and you'll understand why the settlement never materialised.

Clandestine Operations!

Hayburn Wyke **48** is arguably the most attractive cove along the Yorkshire coast. Owned by the National Trust, the adjacent woodland is managed for conservation and is a haven for woodland birds. Hayburn Beck follows the steep valley and emerges onto the beach as an attractive waterfall. The

shore is composed almost entirely of large pebbles, making walking difficult. Accessible only from the Cleveland Way or down winding paths through the ancient woodland, this is not a heavily visited stretch of the coastline.

At first sight this is not a place you would associate with clandestine wartime operations, but in the early hours of July 19th 1917 two Germans disembarked from a submarine, the UB21, and landed on the shore. Apparently their task was to sabotage the coastal railway by blowing up the line, but the operation failed. The men got lost and were later captured. The submarine commander Franz Walther waited off shore for three days before finally abandoning the mission. Naval records are ambiguous – that the Germans landed from the UB21 is not in dispute, but exactly what their objective was is in some doubt. The nearest railway is the line between Scarborough and Whitby; was this of importance for a mission of this nature? It seems unlikely.

Perhaps their aim was similar to that of the Russians over 50 years later, about which there is more certainty. At the height of the Cold War in the late 1960s MI5 was becoming increasingly concerned about the large number of suspected Russian spies in the country. The matter came to a head in 1971 with the defection of Oleg Lyalin, a member of the Soviet Trade Delegation. His defection triggered the implementation of Operation FOOT, resulting in the expulsion of over one hundred Soviet officials.

When debriefed, Lyalin revealed that his main task was to seek suitable landing places along the coast where soviet saboteurs could establish local support groups. These groups would carry out sabotage missions to demoralise the local population. A map marking Hayburn Wyke as a potential landing place made by Lyalin after his defection is still held in the archives of MI5.

It is perhaps surprising that this quiet cove should have been the target for not one, but two covert operations. Maybe the reason lies in the very remoteness of the location? So when you walk through this lovely part of the coast today enjoy the scenery and the wildlife, but keep an eye open for submarines!

Footprints in the Sand

Burniston Bay **H** is a famous location for finding dinosaur footprints in the local sandstones. These date from a time some 180 million years ago when this area was occupied by a huge river delta. Over more recent years hundreds of prints have been found ranging from tiny ones only a few centimetres long to others over a metre in length. Many specimens may now be seen in the Rotunda Museum in Scarborough which you will pass as you progress south.

The museum, opened in 1829, was one of the first purpose-built muesums in the country. It was constructed to a circular design suggested by William Smith, the 'Father of English Geology', who in later life resided in the Scarborough area.

10 Scarborough to Filey

10½ miles (16.7km)
past Cayton Bay

Ascent 1,602 feet (488 metres)
Descent 1,459 feet (445 metres)
Lowest point Scarborough 3 feet (1 metre)
Highest point Osgodby 319 feet (97 metres)

Scarborough's two fine bays are divided by a dramatic headland capped by an ancient castle. Each bay has its own character, North Bay showing a younger face partly fringed with Victorian properties while South Bay, the oldest part of town, shows a more active face with its harbour, shops and amusement arcades. South from the town the Way passes several different bays, each a reflection of the changed geology, before it finally terminates in the long dramatic promontory of Filey Brigg and the end of your Cleveland Way walk.

Where the promenade joins the road **A** it is possible in season to take the open-topped bus which goes from here around the Castle Headland to the South Bay. If you don't feel this is cheating then it makes a very pleasant change and avoids a good length of concrete surface. The advantage of walking, however, is that you can read some excellent interpretative plaques recording the history of the Royal Albert Drive and its continuation, the Marine Drive.

If you are walking the route in spring or early summer you will have good views of the large kittiwake colony nesting

on the cliffs of the headland. There is also a good chance of seeing peregrine falcons which nest here and prey on the kittiwakes.

The Marine Drive was once a toll road and you pass beneath the old toll house as you enter the South Bay **B**. Look out on the right for the house where Richard III is reputed to have stayed in 1484, which is now a restaurant. We know from documentary evidence that Richard was in Scarborough in that year; whether he actually stayed in this house is a matter of debate, but it's a good story!

Continue around the seafront, passing the harbour and the new lifeboat station and beneath the towering edifice of the Grand Hotel. Opened in 1867, it was at that time one of the largest brick built structures in Europe. As you arrive opposite the high level Spa Bridge **C** you have a choice of two routes. If the tide is high it would be advisable to take the high level route.

High level route: Part of the low route may be impassable if the tide is high, in which case turn right under the Spa Bridge and at the next roundabout turn left; after about 50 yards (46m) take the path up through the gardens on the left which will bring you onto the Esplanade. Continue ahead until you reach the prominent Clock Tower. Walk beneath the Clock Tower and down through the gardens, bearing left down the valley and down steps to reach sea level where you reconnect with

the Cleveland Way. Turn right up the limestone track **D**.

Low level route: If the tide is well out continue ahead past the Spa buildings and then around the sea wall to the large, flat area which was once the South Bay seawater bathing pool, the largest in Europe **49**, which

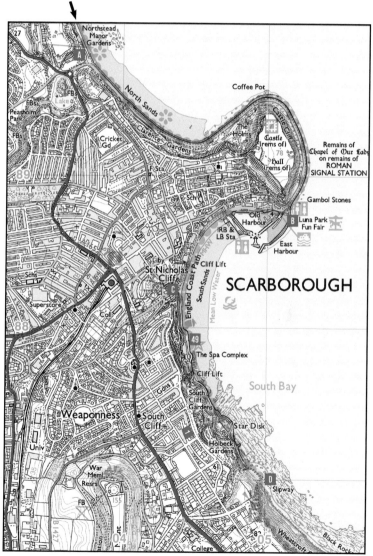

Contours are given in metres
The vertical interval is 10m

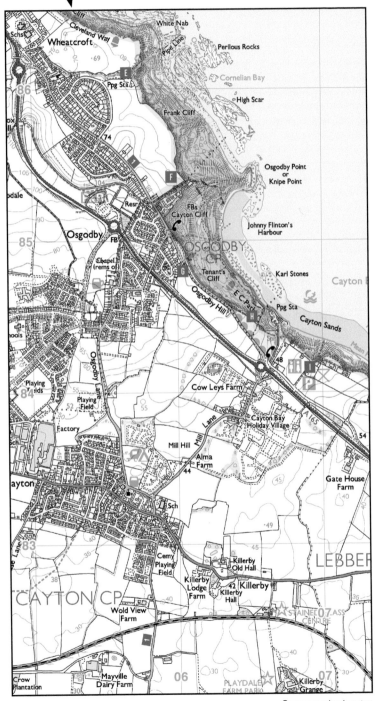

Contours are given in metres
The vertical interval is 10m

closed in the late 1980s. Filled in at great expense, it is now a star disk which apparently shows the northern hemisphere sky at night. You may need to spend some time here if you wish to work out what is where. Just past the star disk the route drops to the beach for a short distance before reaching a wide limestone track that climbs uphill **D**. This was the site of a huge landslip which occurred in June 1993, taking with it a large cliff top hotel, the Holbeck Hall. Built in 1879 as a private residence, the then owner, on being advised that the site might not be safe, reputedly stated that "It will see me out!", and it did!

You are now back on the main route. Towards the top of the hill where the limestone track begins to level out, bear left on a path through the wood which shortly emerges on the cliff top, leading along the edge of the golf course. Can you spot the large topiary rabbit?

If the tide is low as you walk along this next section of the route you will see a large 'South America shaped' cut in the rocks on the shore. Stone was quarried here centuries ago and ferried across the bay to build the early piers of Scarborough harbour.

The path now drops down into a ravine and reaches a broad limestone track which climbs uphill to the right **E**. At the top bear left along the cliff edge, through the bushes and along the field edge. Ahead is a development of bungalows. On reaching them the path turns sharp right **F** uphill to emerge on a road. Turn left and soon after the brow of the hill look out for a sharp left turn **G** onto a footpath which drops steeply down into the woods. At a lower level a path goes straight ahead towards the shore, but you turn sharp right to continue along the lower cliff edge. This whole area is the result of ancient land slipping.

Overlooking the site of the old waterworks, the route now climbs steeply uphill **H**, reaching a hand gate at the top. Turn left through the gate and head downhill to cross a narrow tarmac road (leading to the shore and the old waterworks) and go straight ahead up the other side, emerging once again on the cliff edge. Pass on the seaward side of a small bungalow **I**, cross another path which goes down to the beach, and stay on the cliff edge as the path gradually climbs towards higher cliffs in the distance.

The beach here is littered with the remains of Second World War concrete pillboxes. Cayton Bay was considered a possible easy landing place for German troops and so was heavily defended. The present position of the remains now on the beach or overhanging the cliff top is a good indication of the amount of coastal erosion which has taken place here over the past few decades. From the top of Red Cliff there are extensive views in all directions towards the Yorkshire Wolds, Vale of Pickering and the southern slopes of the North York Moors.

The path stays along the cliff edge as it swings around the headland before climbing gradually to pass in front of a

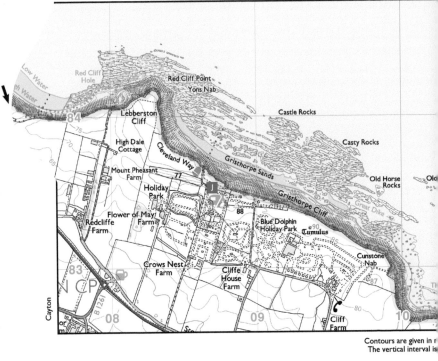

Contours are given in n
The vertical interval is

Yorkshire's annual county Cricket Festival week at Scarborough's North Marine Road ground
– in atmosphere a kind of Lord's Test of the north – invariably attracts large crowds

row of cliff top static caravans **J**. There are many warning notices here about the dangers of sheer cliffs. At the far end of the large caravan site there is a classic view along the cliff line, clearly showing the different strata as they dip towards Filey Brigg. Once around the deep inlet of The Wyke, the end of your long walk comes into view and it's downhill all the way. Pass another rocket brigade practice post and there's the stone obelisk marking the end of the Cleveland Way **50**. Congratulations, you've arrived! But wait, what's this on the other side? Filey Brigg is also the end of The Wolds Way. If you can manage another 79 miles (127km) the Yorkshire Wolds Way National Trail will take you over the rolling Yorkshire Wolds and down to the banks of the mighty Humber estuary – perhaps another day!

rs are given in metres
rtical interval is 10m

Queen of Watering Places

It is no coincidence that nearly all the towns and villages along the Yorkshire coast developed in the lee of a headland. When north-easterly gales sweep down the North Sea, people need all the protection they can get. Scarborough is no exception, with the oldest part of the town sheltered by the massive Castle Headland. Early history here dates back to at least the Bronze Age, with every succeeding age leaving its mark on the town.

Fishing would always have been a major part of the early community activity but today's industry is only a shadow of its former self. The industry which really put the town on the map, tourism, began over 300 years ago with the discovery of an iron-rich spring seeping from the cliffs near to where the Spa was later built. Extolled for its health-giving properties, people were soon flocking to the town to 'take the waters'.

The arrival of the railway from York in 1845 gave a great boost to the tourist trade, seaside holidays became popular and the town expanded rapidly to cater for visitors. The most impressive building of those years was the Grand Hotel under whose towering edifice you walk along the sea front. Raised in 1867, this remarkable building is said to have 365 rooms, 52 chimneys, 12 floors and 4 towers, representing the divisions of the year. The nearby elegant Spa Bridge **C** opened in 1827. In its shadow can be seen the unique Rotunda Museum which opened two years later, built to a design suggested by William Smith, 'Father of English Geology', in order that the geological collections could be displayed in their ascending order of age. It is one of the oldest purpose-built museums in Britain which is still welcoming visitors. Beyond the Spa is the South Cliff Tramway conveying passengers from the Spa to the Esplanade above. This was the first funicular railway to be opened in the country in 1873. After slipping into the doldrums in the 1960s the town has since been rejuvenated to once again become the 'Queen of Watering Places'.

Filey Brigg

If you have the energy, a stroll out along the top of the Brigg is well worth while **50**. Pointing due east seawards, the rocks form the base of the promontory dip from north to south, giving the two sides of the Brigg a marked contrast in scenery. The solid rocks are thickly overlain by glacial boulder clays which on the south side have been deeply eroded into dramatic 'bad land' topography. On a windy day the difference in the sea state on either side of the Brigg can be quite impressive. This is also a classic location for bird watching, with many species of seabird, divers and ducks as well as smaller species which frequent the rough grassland on the Brigg top. With luck you may spot seals or whales offshore.

Part way along the Brigg is a plaque describing the site of a Roman signal station, the last in the line of stations extending from Huntcliff in the north. Once again the remains offer excellent evidence for the high rate of coastal erosion along many parts of the Yorkshire coast. The views from this breezy promontory are extensive. To the south, the wide sandy sweep of Filey Bay gradually gives way to the white chalk cliffs of Speeton and Bempton, another great place for watching birds and the site of the only mainland breeding colony of gannets in England. Further south is the headland of Flamborough while to the north Scarborough, Ravenscar and the north side of Robin Hood's Bay all come into view.

The End of the Line

Of the several coastal resorts along the Yorkshire coast Filey is the smallest, but what it lacks in size it makes up for in attractive buildings and quiet charm. As with all the coastal settlements along the Cleveland Way, Filey evolved in the shelter of a headland. Records suggest that it dates back well over 1000 years and its principal economy was based, unsurprisingly, on fishing. Traditional Yorkshire cobles can still be spotted drawn up on the slipway but sadly not in the numbers seen in the past. Because of the wide extensive beach, the cobles have to be drawn by tractor across the sand, to and from the sea. The development of modern Filey commenced in the early 19th century and, with the arrival of the railway in 1846, the pattern was set for its future prosperity as a tourist resort. A fitting place to end your walk along the Cleveland Way.

Filey Brigg marks the dramatic conclusion of both the Cleveland Way and the Yorkshire Wolds Way National Trails.

PART THREE

Useful Information

Websites

The first source of useful information is the Cleveland Way website at
ⓘ www.nationaltrail.co.uk
Other useful websites include;
ⓘ www.northyorkmoors.org.uk and
ⓘ www.yorkshire.com

Contact the Trail Officer

The quickest way to contact the Trail Officer, Malcolm Hodgson, is via the website, alternatively ring ☎ +44 (0) 1439 772700. email m.hodgson@northyorkmoors.org.uk By post at North York Moors National Park, The Old Vicarage, Bondgate, Helmsley, York, YO62 5BP

Getting to Helmsley

From York: Take the service bus direct to Helmsley or take the train to Scarborough and then the bus to Helmsley.
From Scarborough: Take the service bus direct to Helmsley.
From Hull: Take the ferry bus provided into the city then the train to either Scarborough or York and then bus to Helmsley.
From Newcastle: Take the ferry bus into the city then the train to York and bus to Helmsley.

Return from Filey

To Hull: Take the train or bus, then the ferry bus provided.
To Newcastle: Take the train to Scarborough then onward to York and Newcastle to connect with the ferry bus.

Visit ⓘ www.yorkshiretravel.net
ⓘ www.traveline.info for detailed travel information.

Car Parking

There are numerous car parks on or close to the Cleveland Way. There is often a charge for parking. If you plan to leave your car parked for a number of days, you are advised to inform the local police with full details of the car and your plans for returning.

Accommodation

A detailed guide to accommodation on or near the Way, including B & B, camping sites and hostels, is available on the website www. nationaltrail.co.uk Details of YHA hostels may be obtained at www.yha.org.uk or telephone ☎ 0800 0191 700 or ☎ 01629 592 700 Non-members can stay at a YHA hostel on payment of a small supplement. If planning to 'wild camp' please remember there is a great risk of fire in forest and on moorland. At all times 'wild camping' requires the permission of the landowner or farmer.

Baggage Services

There are several companies which will transfer your luggage between accommodation stops. Details can be found on the website ⓘ www.nationaltrail.co.uk

Information Centres

There are information centres at Sutton Bank, Great Ayton, Guisborough, Saltburn, Staithes, Whitby, Robin Hood's Bay, Ravenscar, Scarborough and Filey. Contact details can be found on the Trail website. Many centres have seasonal opening times.

Equipment & Safety

However you plan to walk the Cleveland Way, ensure that you have suitable equipment. Parts of the route are high and exposed. Strong, comfortable footwear and good waterproofs are essential. The weather can change quickly so be prepared. The route is very well waymarked and you are never very far from a road or habitation; but emergency equipment including a compass, whistle and small first aid kit is strongly recommended. Remember, your safety is your responsibility.

Bibliography

Sampson, Ian, *North York Moors: The Official National Park Guide* (David & Charles, 2001)

Osborne, Roger, *Rocks and Landscape of the North York Moors* (NYMNP Authority, 2010)

Osborne, Roger & Bowden, Alistair, *The Dinosaur Coast* (NYMNP Authority, 2001)

Spratt & Harrison (eds), *Landscape Heritage of the North York Moors* (David & Charles, 1989)

Mead, Harry, *Inside the North York Moors* (David & Charles. 1978) (New ed. Dalesman Publishing Co, 1994)

Mead, Harry, *A Prospect of the North York Moors* (Hutton Press. 2000)

Sykes, Nan, *Wild Plants and their Habitats in the North York Moors* (NYMNP Authority, 1993)

Ordnance Survey Maps

Explorer Maps (scale 1:25,000)

Outdoor Leisure 26 Western area

Outdoor Leisure 27 Eastern area

Comments

Any comments concerning the Cleveland Way should be sent to the Cleveland Way Project Officer, North York Moors National Park Authority, The Old Vicarage, Bondgate, Helmsley, York. YO62 5BP

Useful Information

The Official Guides to all

Cotswold Way
Anthony Burton

100 miles of quintessentially
English landscape

ISBN 978-1-84513-570-5

Cleveland Way
Alan Staniforth

Over 100 miles of magnificent walking
on the North York Moors

ISBN 978-1-78131-503-3

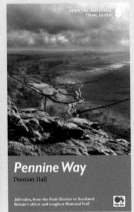

Pennine Way
Damian Hall

268 miles, from the Peak District to Scotland.
Britain's oldest and toughest National Trail

ISBN 978-1-78131-565-1

Yorkshire Wolds Way
Tony Gowers
and Roger Ratcliffe

A superbly tranquil walk through
the unspoilt chalk hills of Yorkshire

ISBN 978-1-78131-568-2

**Pembrokeshire
Coast Path**
Wales Coast Path: St Dogmaels to Amroth
Brian John

ISBN 978-1-84513-572-9

South Downs Way
Paul Millmore

100 miles of glorious chalk downland
for the walker, cyclist and horse rider

ISBN 978-1-78131-563-7

Hadrian's Wall Path
Anthony Burton

Follow the Roman Wall
from coast to coast

ISBN 978-1-78131-571-2

The Ridgeway
Anthony Burton

87 miles of downland walking
from Wiltshire to the Chilterns

ISBN 978-1-78131-573-6

North Downs Way
Colin Saunders

Follow the chalk ridge across South-East
England all the way to the sea

ISBN 978-1-78131-500-2

# of Britain's National Trails

Thames Path
in the Country
David Sharp and Tony Gowers
From the source to Hampton Court

ISBN 978-1-78131-575-0

Thames Path
in London
Phoebe Clapham
From Hampton Court to Crayford Ness:
50 miles of historic riverside walk

ISBN 978-1-78131-754-9

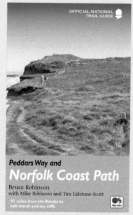

Peddars Way and
Norfolk Coast Path
Bruce Robinson
with Mike Robinson and Tim Lidstone-Scott
92 miles from the Brecks to
salt marsh and sea cliffs

ISBN 978-1-78131-566-8

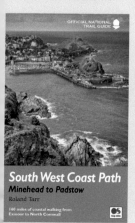

South West Coast Path
Minehead to Padstow
Roland Tarr
160 miles of coastal walking from
Exmoor to North Cornwall

ISBN 978-1-78131-564-4

South West Coast Path
Padstow to Falmouth
John Macadam
From golden beaches to rugged coves
around Britain's southernmost tip

ISBN 978-1-78131-580-4

Offa's Dyke Path
Ernie and Kathy Kay and Mark Richards
Edited by Tony Gowers
Follow the ancient earthwork for 177 miles
from the Severn Estuary to the Irish Sea

ISBN 978-1-78131-066-3

South West Coast Path
Falmouth to Exmouth
Roland Tarr
From St Mawes Castle to the Exe Estuary –
179 miles of dramatic and historic coastline

ISBN 978-1-78131-579-8

South West Coast Path
Exmouth to Poole
Roland Tarr
From Jane Austen's Cobb to Lulworth Cove
– over 100 miles of historic coastline

ISBN 978-1-78131-567-5

Other guide books from

Aurum Press

The Capital Ring
Colin Saunders

78 miles of green corridor encircling inner London

ISBN 978-1-78131-569-9

The London Loop
Colin Saunders

150 miles of secret countryside to walk in a green corridor around London

ISBN 978-1-78131-561-3

West Highland Way
Anthony Burton

94 miles of Scottish moor and mountain in Britain's most spectacular long-distance walk

ISBN 978-1-78131-576-7

The Coast to Coast Walk
Martin Wainwright

The classic high-level walk from Irish Sea to North Sea

ISBN 978-1-84513-560-6

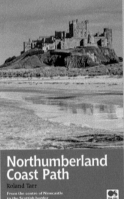

Northumberland Coast Path
Roland Tarr

From the centre of Newcastle to the Scottish border

ISBN 978-1-78131-562-0

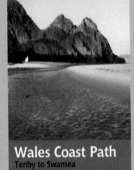

Wales Coast Path
Tenby to Swansea
Chris Moss

Endless sandy beaches and the beautiful Gower Peninsula

ISBN 978-1-78131-067-0

Somerset Coast Path
Damian Hall

121 miles of beautiful scenery, history and surprises

ISBN 978-1-78131-185-1

Camino de Santiago
Sergi Ramis

The ancient Way of Saint James pilgrimage route from the French Pyrenees to Santiago de Compostela

ISBN 978-1-78131-223-0

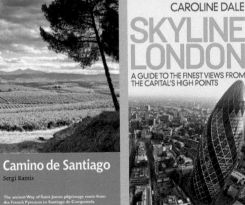

CAROLINE DALE

SKYLINE LONDON
A GUIDE TO THE FINEST VIEWS FROM THE CAPITAL'S HIGH POINTS

ISBN 978-1-84513-762-5